# 44 EZ Solutions to Stretch and Conserve Your DOLLAR

# 44 EZ Solutions to Stretch and Conserve Your DOLLAR

Jerry LePre

SELFHELP SUCCESS BOOKS

Gretna 2009

**Library of Congress Cataloging-in-Publication Data**

LePre, Jerry.
44 EZ solutions to stretch and conserve your dollar / Jerry LePre.
p. cm.
Includes bibliographical references.
ISBN 978-1-935235-05-7
1. Finance, Personal. 2. Investments. I. Title. II. Title: Forty-four EZ solutions to stretch and conserve your dollar.
HG179.L448 2009
332.024—dc22

2009032102

Selfhelp Success, Selfhelp Success Books, and are imprints of Selfhelp Success Books, L.L.C.

Printed in the United States of America

Published by Selfhelp Success Books, L.L.C.
900 Burmaster Street, Gretna, Louisiana 70053

*This book is dedicated to*
*E.Z., Elbert Zane Brown III.*
*E.Z. will be remembered as a godly man*
*who overcame so many challenges in life*
*to become a respected and loved father, husband, brother,*
*son, counselor, mentor, and friend.*
*During his short life, he inspired so many to overcome*
*personal challenges.*
*He never gave up. His family always came first.*
*His memory will continue to serve as an inspiration for*
*all who face challenges in life and dare to rise above. His*
*legacy of love will endure through his work, children,*
*wife, sister, and mother, who cherished him.*

*I use his life as an example to live by*
*for the rest of my life.*

# Contents

# Introduction

Despite the bailout "rescue" bill and stimulus packages passed by Congress in 2008 and 2009, the U.S. economy is still in a lot of trouble. In fact, the current economic times, which are often considered a recession, could be described as a controlled depression.

When you combine this financial uncertainty with inflation, many American families are unable to meet basic monthly expenses. Some surveys have indicated that nearly 83 percent of us have nothing left at the end of the month. In fact, a survey conducted by AARP showed that almost one out of five of baby boomers have cut or stopped their retirement savings.

One of the major causes of our financial challenges is debt. In fact, credit card debt grew about $70 billion during July 2007 and July 2008, according to the Federal Reserve. To make matters worse, a recent survey by Standard & Poor's revealed that one in five credit card holders are having difficulty paying their monthly statements.

In these desperate times of financial survival, we must, more than ever, get the most from every precious penny we earn. We work hard for our money; now we must use it more intelligently and efficiently. The challenge may seem overwhelming, but the answer may be simpler than you think. *44 EZ Solutions to Stretch and Conserve Your Dollar* can help you survive and thrive with practical and easy-to-implement tactics. By achieving only a few of my action items, you will have empowered yourself to become financially free.

My book is designed to increase your ability to create, accumulate, manage, and conserve assets (wealth). I begin by discussing seven different but related strategies that need analysis, tactical planning, coordination, and, most of all, ACTION.

**THE SEVEN BUILDING BLOCK STRATEGIES:**

1. Develop and Follow a Financial Freedom Plan
2. Pay Less and Conserve More

3. Reorganize Existing Debt
4. Maximize Insurance while Minimizing Cost
5. Reduce Your Taxes
6. Invest in Your Future
7. Keep Your Wealth: Estate Conservation

The first strategy features the *Financial Freedom Planner*, which functions as your financial game plan. This serves as your starting point to form a plan once you set your financial priorities.

Strategies 2 through 5 offer more than 200 tried and true tips to reduce expenses, create and keep wealth, and increase your disposable income. Such methods include convenient ways to lower utility bills, insurance premiums, gasoline costs, and grocery expenses, just to name a few.

Other tactics will help you effectively negotiate your next vehicle purchase, pay off credit card debt, stand up to sales pressure, and lower your income tax obligation. My helpful concepts are designed to create a cash surplus at the end of the month when all of your bills are paid.

In the sixth stratagem, you will learn how to wisely invest your newfound wealth in order to make it grow.

Finally, the last strategy reveals plans to help you conserve your legacy. In other words, it can help you *preserve your wealth* for generations to come.

*Financial freedom* is possible for everyone if you are dedicated enough to take the time to plan, disciplined enough to implement it, and wise enough to monitor your results. It may take a little bit of sacrifice on your part, but the peace and joy of being financially free is well worth the effort. Sacrifices, even small ones, develop character and teach you to appreciate a balanced lifestyle.

*Stay focused on your vision of financial freedom.*

*Author's Note* This book is written and designed solely as an educational tool. Its use is intended to provide information, not advice for specific individuals or situations. When used properly, it will give you the insight needed to effectively use the advice of competent financial advisors. It should not be relied upon as the sole basis for investment decisions or financial decisions of any other kind.

CHAPTER 1

# Develop and Follow a Financial Freedom Plan

In my years of financial counseling, I discovered that only a few people are aware of their month-to-month financial position. The main reason being that most individuals and families are not actively following an updated or realistic financial game plan with priorities suited to their needs and abilities. In my experience, most individuals and families do not have any form of a *Financial Freedom Plan*, commonly known as a budget, to control and allocate their spending. This reactionary method, which responds to financial crises rather than preparing for them, eventually leads to economic failure. The first step toward financial victory begins with the creation of a realistic *financial plan.*

Solutions for a Successful Financial Plan:

1. Redefine Spending Priorities
2. Establish Realistic Monthly Expense Objectives
3. Follow a Financial Freedom Plan

**Solution 1: Redefine Spending Priorities**

When you put your desires and luxuries first, your number one priority is to get the best, most expensive items available on the market, whether it's groceries or cars, pencils or computers, regardless of repercussions. This behavior is a reaction to your addiction to sales pressure designed to draw you away from your resolve and help you rationalize unnecessary and unwise purchases. *No money down! No credit refused!* Without the right priorities, good people fall into *unnecessary debt* and *financial bondage.*

Before you can establish your financial plan, you must first begin by defining then organizing your priorities. These priorities will become the roadmap that defines your financial goals and transforms them into reality. Without the right priorities, your financial dreams will remain only in your imagination.

Your plan for after-tax dollars should be divided into seven sections. The importance of offerings and gifts is subject to the importance placed on them by the giver, thus this section is unnumbered. The next six are listed in order of importance, based on their urgency and necessity.

Priorities:

Offerings and Gifts
1. Necessities
2. Shelter
3. Transportation
4. Savings and Investments
5. Lifestyle
6. Luxuries

OFFERINGS AND GIFTS
1. NECESSITIES
   - Food
   - Clothing
   - Home Furnishings: Furniture, Appliances / Electronics
   - Medical expenses
   - Staples: Paper Products, Cleaning Supplies, Toiletries, Etc.
2. SHELTER
   - Mortgage / Rent
   - Home Insurance
   - Property Taxes
   - Utilities
   - Telephone (cell phone if primary phone)
   - Repairs
   - Maintenance / Miscellaneous
3. TRANSPORTATION
   - Vehicle Payment(s)
   - Gasoline
   - Car Insurance

Repairs
Licenses / Taxes
Maintenance / Miscellaneous

4. SAVINGS/INVESTMENTS
Regular Savings
Emergency Fund
Life and Disability Insurance
Retirement Fund
Low- and Medium-Risk Investments
5. LIFESTYLE
Education
Leisure / Entertainment
Grooming
Recreational Clubs
Health and Fitness Clubs
6. LUXURIES

**Solution 2: Establish Realistic Monthly Expense Objectives**

Before you proceed to the Financial Freedom Planner, you must establish realistic anticipated values for your various monthly expenditures. You must first review your current financial position by listing all fixed short- and long-term fiscal obligations along with variable expenses. Since your fixed payments cannot change in the near future, it is important to search for ways to reduce your variable expenses.

Several tactics designed to achieve this objective are found in the remaining *building block strategies*. Thus, much of your plan may change when you have the information necessary to lower expenses. The key to a successful Financial Freedom Plan is to make it flexible enough to respond to emergencies and other changes in income or expenses.

If you are having trouble determining any monthly expense, review your bank statements for the past few months and use prior monthly payments to determine how to plan. You may want to adjust this average due to inflation or cost increases.

*Note*: Here, as in the original list of priorities, offerings and gifts are undefined because of their subjective nature.

General Percentage Guidelines:

| Spending Category | Low % | Avg % | High % |
|---|---|---|---|
| Necessities | 20% | 25% | 30% |
| Shelter | 25% | 32.5% | 35% |
| Transportation | 15% | 20% | 25% |
| Savings/Investments | 7.5% | 12.5% | 15% |
| Lifestyle | 5% | 7.5% | 10% |
| Luxuries | 0.0% | 2.5% | 5% |
| Offerings/Gifts | ? | ? | ? |

**Solution 3: Follow a Financial Freedom Plan**

*Tactic 3a Focus on Financial Freedom Circle*

The monthly *Financial Freedom Planner* is different from any budgeting method you have previously seen or used for achieving financial goals. This concept is based on a spherical shape as the point of reference for all of your financial records and decisions.

This shape is used to represent my financial philosophy for the following five reasons:

1. Since every point of a sphere's surface is an equal distance from the center, it represents the idea that every aspect of our planning should revolve around our life-changing experiences. (The changes we face in life, such as marriage, births, deaths, divorces, job loss, sickness, etc., affect how we make our financial decisions.)
2. A circle has no end. It continuously goes around and around. This symbolizes the ongoing nature of our financial responsibility and decision making.
3. The pie chart in the background of the Financial Freedom Planner (see page 92) clearly shows the monthly allotment for each priority. Since offerings and gifts are determined by the giver, this priority is not included.
4. The surface area of this circle is shaped by our current financial conditions. The larger the circle, the more resources are available to us. We should strive to increase the size of that circle by realizing our potential resources.
5. When it comes to our finances, if we keep doing what we have been, we will keep getting the same results. We have the freedom to

change our thinking, decisions, focus, and actions, and therefore to effect positive change in our finances. Positive change frees us from going around in unproductive circles.

The Financial Freedom Planner is found on page 92.

*Tactic 3b Start an Envelope System*

To reinforce a written plan you can use the old-fashioned envelope system. Basically, for each paycheck you receive place cash into seven envelopes, one for each of the seven monthly expense categories. When the funds in a given envelope disappear, you either have to take from another category or wait until the next pay period to make the purchase. This method prevents you from spending more than you make, thus helping you to avoid debt.

CHAPTER 2

# Pay Less and Conserve More

Surveys indicate that more than four out of five Americans are not able to pay basic monthly bills. Once you have a Financial Freedom Plan, the next step toward financial freedom is learning how to get the most for your dollar. The second building block strategy offers over 150 action items that enable you to reduce expenses and resist the draw of sales enticements.

**Solution 4: Get the Most for Your Dollar**

It is very important for consumers to get the most value for their dollar when they make purchases.

The following techniques will help you obtain the greatest value for your money:

- *Look for Sales*—The difference between an item's retail price and its sale price varies as much as 50 percent from store to store. During liquidation sales this discount could be even higher. A wise bargain hunter shops at several stores and waits for periodic sales before purchasing any item by monitoring the newspaper and other media to learn when the sales occur. In general, most stores have sales for every season. However, the best way to know of a coming sale is to develop a close relationship with a sales consultant.
- *Buy Your Item the Night before a Sale Begins*—If you make a purchase the night before a sale starts, most stores will apply the sales price to your purchase. This way you not only avoid the crowd but you also have a full selection to choose from.
- *Plan Your Purchases in Advance*—By anticipating your needs, you are able to wait for sales to make purchases. Create a shopping

list to eliminate the urgency of making full-price purchases out of necessity.

• *Buy Quality, Lesser Known Products Instead of Expensive Name Brands*—Flashy commercials and celebrity endorsements have nothing to do with quality. In fact, several well-known products are often inferior to unknown brands that put their emphasis on quality work in lieu of persuasive commercials. An educated shopper has researched various consumer product ratings before making any large purchases. Once you determine the best brand, then look for the best price.

• *Use Coupons*—If you diligently seek and use the hundreds of valuable discount coupons that are available, you can save hundreds of dollars annually.

• *Contemplate Buying Slightly Damaged Items*—Many large stores, particularly outlet stores, offer substantial savings on slightly damaged goods. Often, the only difference readily apparent from the regular items is the lower price.

• *Consider Purchasing Used Items*—Before buying any new product, look through the classified section of your newspaper to see if you could purchase the same item used. This could yield tremendous savings on some items. However, remember warranties usually are not transferred in the sale of a previously owned item.

• *Use Mature Citizen Discounts*—Several companies offer adults 55 years and older substantial discounts on products, services, insurance premiums, and meals.

• *Consider Renting Instead of Buying*—If you do not intend to use a product frequently, it may save you money to rent the item. A wise consumer never pays to have dust collect on his or her possessions.

• *Get a Library Card*—Instead of buying books, CDs, or DVDs, use the library's huge selection, which includes popular titles.

• *Negotiate Prices*—Some retail outlets allow the consumer to negotiate final prices with the owner or sales manager of the store. Small stores, particularly sole-proprietors, may negotiate if they believe they may lose a sale. Don't be timid. Be firm and determined when finalizing a price. If the terms are not right, walk away.

• *Participate in Discount Buyer Groups*—You may consider

joining one of several buyer networks. These associations allow their members to directly purchase wholesale products and other items with substantial discounts. In some cases, members receive compensation or a bonus for enlisting new recruits.

- *Contemplate Using the Barter System*—Instead of cash, some merchants may accept barter. Before the invention of currency, bartering was the only means of trade. Find out if your community has a "Barter Club" or start your own.

**Solution 5: Pay with Cash or Use Credit to Your Benefit**

*Tactic 5a Avoid Long-Term Credit Card Debt by Using Cash*

All your effort in and savings from Solution 4 could be wasted if you make your purchases with long-term credit instead of paying cash. In fact, you may end up paying over twice the cost of the original price due to accumulated interest.

If you pay only a $15 monthly minimum payment on a credit card balance of $750 at 19.8 percent interest, it will take you 106 months to payoff your balance. To make matters worse, if you continue to make additional purchases on your card in excess of your monthly principal payment, you create a perpetual balance that is never paid off.

In this scenario, instead of paying $750 for the item you pay approximately $1,600, of which almost $850 is interest. Solution 18 (page 35) shows how to eliminate 80 percent of this interest by repaying existing credit card debt with accelerated payments.

*Tactic 5b Plastic Surgery: Use One Credit Card to Your Benefit*

Years ago, Americans carried photographs of their families in wallets. Now, too many don't have any room left in their wallet since it is bulging with plastic money. In fact, the average American has 10 active credit cards. In order to avoid temptation, a wise consumer should perform *plastic surgery* on their finances and cut up all but one credit card. However, don't cancel unused cards since this would hurt your credit rating. The one credit card you keep should have a competitive interest rate and reward features, such as airline miles or cash back.

Your one major credit card should be limited to the following specific objectives:

• *Financial Guarantor*—Most reputable corporations require credit cards to secure reservations and guarantee payment of services. Consequently, your credit card acts as a financial guarantor when renting cars and making hotel reservations, but once the service has been rendered you are often free to pay cash rather than charge your credit card.

• *Credit Reference*—A second benefit credit cards provide is a credit reference.

• *Emergency Funds*—Your card should only be used in case of an emergency.

• *Earn Money*—If you are disciplined, you can earn money or other benefits by using your credit card wisely and effectively.

• *Less Hassle*—When you use a credit card you may find it easier to get credit for returns and exchanges without hassles or delays. Your credit card may offer cash back or other rewards for purchases, such as air miles.

*Tactic 5c Beware of the Teaser Rate*

The biggest credit card trap is the zero or low percent interest options offered for a short period of time when you transfer your balance. With balance transfers of this type, an initial fee of three percent is usually charged to the entire amount of the transfer. Thus, if the old account balance is $1,000, the new account balance will be $1,030 since it reflects the balance transferred plus the $30 fee. The credit card company profits when you don't pay off the balance during a specific timeframe, after which point the interest rate increases drastically. Some cards may even accrue interest, which is applied to your account if the balance is not paid off by the time the special offer expires. In addition, if you use your card for other, higher-interest charges, your payments are applied first to the lower interest balance until it is paid off. Thus, you begin to owe even larger sums on the higher-interest balance.

## Solution 6: Disconnect Landline Telephone (If You Have a Cell Phone)

If you have a cell phone, consider using it as your only phone.

By disconnecting your landline telephone, you could save as much as $50 per month. However, use your plan wisely to avoid additional airtime charges. Also, consider the advantages of a family plan.

**Solution 7: Get Your Credit Report in Shape**

Your three-digit credit score is one of the most important numbers in your life. Basically, your score is a snapshot of the way you handle your money. It gives creditors insight into how you pay your bills, how you've handled long- and short-term credit in the past, and negative events in your financial life, such as bankruptcy or repossessions. A high score gets you a preferred interest rate when borrowing money, while a low score places you in either the sub-prime market or in a position where you cannot get credit on any terms. When it comes to major purchases such as a home or vehicle, this could mean thousands of dollars saved in interest for having an excellent credit score or thousands of dollars lost for a poor credit score.

Here are six ways to try to fix your credit:

1. *Obtain Your Credit Report*—You are entitled to one free report per year. Visit www.annualcreditreport.com to obtain your copy. It is also available from the main credit reporting agencies—Equifax, Experian, and TransUnion.

2. *Check for Errors*—In addition to checking your personal information, review all of the accounts listed on your report to locate duplicate entries and items that shouldn't be there. You must notify the credit bureau in writing of any errors you find.

3. *Dispute Negative Items that Are Not Accurate*—You should contact creditors who reported negative issues to the bureau to dispute contested items.

4. *Pay Small Disputed Items*—If you can afford the payment, it is better to pay a creditor for a small disputed item than have your credit damaged.

5. *Pay Bills on Time*—This is the best way to establish excellent credit.

6. *Never Cancel Cards or Reduce Limits*— Your best credit score occurs when your debt utilization ratio is 10 to 20 percent. The debt utilization ratio is the amount of credit used as compared to

the total amount of credit available. Thus, if your limit is $10,000 you should have a balance between $1,000 and $2,000.

**Solution 8: Don't Buy Impulsively! Avoid Sales Pressure**

Consumers are constantly being bombarded by advertisements. Commercials, billboards, flyers, and print ads are encountered everywhere you turn. They are seen and/or heard on the television, radio, newspapers, magazines, sports stadiums, and clothing. No one is safe from the *advertiser*.

Since you can't escape the constant badgering of persuasive propaganda, it is important that you learn how to defend yourself from this unyielding sales pressure. Learn all the facts before you buy. Read the fine print. Remember that the salesperson (in most cases) only gets paid if you buy.

- *Never Purchase Anything Immediately After Viewing Advertisement*—Put off the buying decision for at least three days, then evaluate whether or not you really want to spend your money on it. Most of the time, you will be surprised how your obsession with something will decrease after 72 hours.
- *Discuss All Purchases with Your Spouse*—Spouses have a tremendous ability to get your spending priorities back in focus. Singles should discuss purchases with their parents, siblings, or responsible friends.
- *Take Charge of the Buying Process*—Consumers often forget they control the outcome of all sales presentations. If you feel pressured by a sales person, tell them you are not ready to buy today.
- *Ask for All Warranties, Guarantees, and Promises in Writing*—If a salesperson won't put their enticements in writing, don't buy the product or service.
- *Evaluate Extended Service Contracts*—Before buying such a plan, first find out what the manufacturer warranty entails. Then compare the cost of the extended service contract (ESC) to anticipated repairs. Don't feel rushed, you have 30 days to make a decision.
- *Take Control: Refurbish, Revive, and Renew*—Before buying something new, try to refresh what you already have. Update old items with a new look or modify them to fit your current needs. This can be done by refinishing, painting, or modifying old pieces of

furniture. You can give clothes a new look with accessories. Remember that your junk could be made into a unique treasure for far less than the cost of a replacement. Let your imagination go to work.

**Solution 9: Lower Utility Bills**

The following tactics can drastically reduce your monthly electric and gas bills.

*Tactic 9a Reduce Usage of Standby Energy*

Standby energy, the energy used by all of our electrical gadgets when not in use, can account for as much as 10 percent of our home energy consumption. Unplugging infrequently used items and plugging frequently used items (televisions, cable boxes, DVD players, chargers, and small appliances without clocks) into a power strip that can be switched off when not in use, can save up to $75 annually.

*Tactic 9b Lower Climate Control Bills*

Heating and cooling are your two biggest energy investments, since climate control represents more than half of your average monthly electric bill. Not surprisingly, these are also areas where you can save a lot of money through smart energy conservation.

The following measures conserve money and minimize loss of heated or cooled air:

- Use a programmable thermostat to control your home's temperature. Every degree of difference between your home's temperature and the atmosphere adds about five percent to your energy bill. During the summer, set it to78 degrees when you are home and 80 degrees when you are out. During the winter, set the thermostat to 68 degrees when at home and 66 degrees when out.
- Install insulation, weather stripping, and attic ventilation.
- Install storm windows and doors that reduce loss of climate-controlled air by up to 20 percent.
- Install adequate insulation: R-30 insulation in the ceiling, R-18 in new walls, R-13 in existing walls, and R-19 under the floor.
- Caulk all cracks between door and window frames.

• Don't block vents or heat registers with curtains, shades, or furniture.
• Check air conditioning and furnace filters every 30 days to determine if they need to be cleaned or replaced. Dirty filters strain your appliances, increasing the energy necessary to function.
• When painting your home or replacing the roof, choose a color appropriate to the climate where you live. Dark colors absorb heat, which lowers your heating bill in winter but increases your cooling bill in summer. The reverse is true for light colors.
• Your cooling and heating systems should be inspected and cleaned by a professional each spring and fall, respectively.
• Keep exterior and attic doors closed so air does not escape.

The following measures reduce the loss of cooled air:

• In summer, close your shades and draperies during the day to keep the heat out of your home. Awnings also help to block the sun.
• Locate your cooling units on the shady side of your home, possibly under a shade tree, instead of in direct sunlight. This reduces sun exposure and therefore overheating.
• Check air ducts for tight joints and good insulation. Cold air wasted in a hot attic costs money.
• Keep air circulating with a ceiling, oscillating, or box fan. A good fan enables you to leave your thermostat at a higher setting, thereby decreasing the energy it uses.
• Reduce heat generation by turning off unnecessary lights and appliances.
• To avoid interior humidity, conduct moisture-generating jobs like mopping, dish washing, and laundering in the cooler early morning or nighttime hours.
• When purchasing a new air conditioning unit, check the energy efficiency rating. The higher the rating, the more efficient the unit. Also, buy a unit with the correct capacity for your home's size.

The following measures reduce the loss of heated air:

• Use sweaters and blankets as alternatives to increasing the temperature of the thermostat.
• During daylight, open shades and draperies to let sunlight warm

your home. At night, close your window coverings to keep heat inside.

- Close dampers and block flues when your fireplace is not in use.

*Tactic 9c Lower Water Heating Bills*

After heating and cooling, maintaining hot water represents about one fourth of your energy expense.

To save hot water:

- Take quick showers instead of a bath.
- Install a water control valve in the showerhead to reduce hot water use from anywhere between five and 15 gallons per minute to between two and three gallons per minute.
- Fill your washer and dishwasher to capacity. A full load requires no more energy or hot water than a partial load.
- Wrap your water heater with insulation to increase its efficiency by more than 10 percent.
- Turn the water heater off when you leave home for long periods.
- Prevent hot water from going down the drain by fixing dripping faucets. A hot water leak that fills an ordinary cup in 10 minutes wastes more than 3,000 gallons of hot water annually.
- Set the thermostat on your water heater as low as possible, following the guidelines of your dishwasher's owner's manual.
- Close the drain on the sink basin when shaving. You can pour as many as six gallons of hot water down the drain during a five-minute shave.

*Tactic 9d Lower Laundry Energy Bills*

Today's washers and dryers are more energy-efficient than older models, but they still require proper use to conserve as much as possible.

To reduce energy spent on laundry:

- Use your washer and dryer only when you have a full load, but don't overload them.
- Use cold water whenever possible for washing and always for rinsing. This conserves the energy of your water heater.

- Clean your dryer's lint filter after every load.
- Dry several loads in succession to maintain heat levels.
- Don't over dry your clothes.

*Tactic 9e Lower Kitchen Energy Bills*

There are more high-energy appliances in the kitchen than anywhere else in your home. Thus, managing energy use in your kitchen is one of the best ways to save money.

To reduce energy use in the kitchen:

- Locate your refrigerator away from heat sources (like the range).
- Close your refrigerator door tightly. Check and replace worn gaskets (stripping around refrigerator door).
- Set the refrigerator temperature between 37 and 42 degrees, and the freezer at zero degrees.
- Turn the refrigerator dial two or three settings warmer when away longer than two days.
- Open the refrigerator door as little as possible.
- Keep all liquids covered to prevent vapors that increase the compressor's workload.
- Clean condenser coils annually. Dirt and dust cover the coils and cause less efficient operation.
- Defrost your refrigerator before the ice deposit exceeds ¼ inch thick.
- Manual defrost refrigerators use less energy than frost-free models.
- Chest-type freezers use less energy than upright freezers.
- Most side-by-side refrigerator/freezers use 45 percent more energy than over-under two-door models.
- Prepare several meals on one day and freeze them for later consumption. This saves time and electric/gas costs.
- Use energy saving settings on appliances.
- Save time and energy by using the microwave oven, crock-pot, grill, toaster, and pressure cooker in lieu of the conventional oven.
- Use pots with tight-fitting lids that hold in heat in order to cook food faster and more efficiently, thereby reducing the energy expended in the process.
- Use as little water as possible when cooking.

• Do not pre-heat the oven for foods that take an hour or more to cook.
• Cook food that requires similar heat levels at the same time in the oven.
• Lower the oven setting by 25 degrees and bake food in heat-retaining ceramic or glass containers.
• Open the oven door as little as possible, relying instead on a timer to tell you when food is nearly done.
• Use your dishwasher only when you have a full load.

*Tactic 9f Lower Lightning Bills*

Even though lighting only accounts for about six percent of your energy bill, a wise consumer can lower this margin and amass significant savings.

To decrease energy expended on lighting:

• Turn off lights in unoccupied rooms.
• Cleaning bulbs and lamp shades regularly can increase light by 30 percent.
• Fluorescent lamps give five times more light and last 10 times longer than incandescent bulbs. They also give off less heat.
• Use high wattage bulbs only where you need bright light. Otherwise, always use a bulb with low wattage and more lumens. Remember the higher the wattage the greater the use of electricity. Also, the more lumens per watt, the higher the bulb's efficiency.
• Dimmer switches control brightness according to necessity. When brightness is not a priority you can save energy by dimming the lights.
• Use sodium vapor lamps in outdoor lighting. They use less energy and last longer than incandescent bulbs.

*Tactic 9g Don't Needlessly Leave the TV On*

This is a pointless waste of energy. Simply turn the television off when you stop watching.

**Solution 10: Decrease Gasoline Consumption**

There are several simple things that you can do to reduce your monthly gasoline bill:

• Eliminate or consolidate short trips.

- Schedule several trips in the same vicinity for one outing.
- Use the lowest grade of gasoline recommended for your car.
- Check your tire pressure. This affects the mileage you get per gallon of gasoline.
- Use self-service gasoline pumps.
- Use car pools and public transformation.
- Do not drive over 55 miles per hour. Excessive speed decreases your gas mileage.
- Avoid abrupt stops and starts.
- Limit air conditioner or heater use.

**Solution 11: Save Money on Your Next Vehicle**

Next to your home, the second largest purchase that most people make is their vehicle. These proactive suggestions can make acquiring your next car a positive economic venture. They will give you the knowledge you need to make the best decision by doing more than just taking a test drive.

Things to consider when buying:

- Consider buying a demo or used vehicle between one and three model years old, since first-year depreciation is tremendous.
- If you must buy a new vehicle, research the dealer cost and offer no more than $200 over invoice. There are books, web sites, and buyers' clubs that offer updated cost information to identify the dealer invoice. The dealer receives bonuses and incentives to make sales that exceed the $200 markup.
- Never lease a vehicle unless it is used for business. However, if you must lease, never agree to a contract for less than 48 months. Since you never earn equity, think of your payment as a perpetually fixed monthly payment adjusted every four years for inflation. A lease can be a trap, especially an open-ended lease. Make sure you have a closed-end lease with an agreed upon final payment. Beware, both forms of leases have excess mileage charges.
- Consider buying a hybrid to receive tax credit up to $7,500. The credits are based on battery capacity rather than electric range, but range increases with capacity.

Things to consider when financing:

- A used vehicle should not be financed for longer than 30 months, and a new vehicle should not be financed for more than 48 months. If possible, make a 20 percent down payment.
- Beware, credit life insurance offered by dealers is excessively expensive.
- If you make a small down payment, purchase gap coverage, since the amount you owe on your vehicle is often greater than its value. In the event of a total loss, your insurance carrier is obligated to pay you only the market value of your vehicle. Your insurance claim payment could be less than your actual payoff. Gap coverage will pay the difference.
- Consider the pros and cons of an extended warranty.

Things to consider when purchasing a used vehicle:

- Check the maintenance record of the vehicle before buying a used vehicle. It is important that routine oil changes and tune-ups were done as recommended.
- Check the odometer reading for the mileage of the vehicle you are considering buying. This should average less than 15,000 miles per year. If the average exceeds this amount, determine if this is highway mileage, which is less taxing on the engine.
- Ask a trusted mechanic to examine the vehicle.
- Insist that the seller provide you with at least a one-year or 12,000-mile warranty.

Things to consider during negotiations, trade-ins, and other miscellany pertaining to a vehicle purchase:

- Check the sticker price for unnecessary charges. This includes dealer preparation and unwanted options and accessories. If the car has an option you don't want, don't buy the car. Have the dealer order another that fits your needs and budget. Since it is important to sell the cars and trucks on the lot, the dealership may choose to include these options at little or no cost instead of ordering a less-equipped version.
- Compare the vehicle's sticker price with other similar models listed elsewhere.

• Find the consumer rating of selected vehicle for repairs, customer satisfaction, and value retention.
• Ask friends and family who own a similar model about their experience with the car.
• Compare the gas mileage to your current vehicle.
• Rent a similarly equipped model for a weekend to see if you are satisfied with it.
• Ask your insurance agent for a quote. Keep in mind that the cost of damage coverage varies by vehicle. (See Solution 25, page 46.)
• Check the retail, trade-in, and wholesale values of your current vehicle for its trade-in potential.
• Don't combine the negotiations to purchase your new vehicle with the discussions of your trade-in. These are two separate deals. You should make the best deal on your new purchase before negotiating your trade-in. Compare the dealer's offer to the vehicle's value as found in your research. If the offer is too low and the dealership refuses to negotiate an acceptable price, consider handling your vehicle's sale yourself.

## Solution 12: Become a Wise Gourmet

*Tactic 12a Plan Your Meals and Grocery Shopping Trips*

The best way to become a wise gourmet is to follow these strategies when grocery shopping:

• Plan your weekly meals in order to make an adequate grocery list.
• Check your pantry, refrigerator, and freezer to determine if you already have items on your list in order to avoid buying duplicates.
• Divide your groceries into the following groups: meats, staples, canned goods, fresh fruits and vegetables, deserts, drinks, and other. Determine what are necessities and what are luxury items.
• Bring a calculator with you to the supermarket. You will use this to determine how discounts affect the actual cost per unit, for example cost per ounce. Calculating cost per unit reveals the difference in actual price for a standard amount of product, because frequently the larger the quantity, the smaller the cost.
• Stick to your list.

• Use manufacturer and grocery store coupons. When using coupons, select the smallest size of the product to take advantage of the absolute lowest cost per unit.
• Compare the company-brand products' prices to the national brands' prices by checking the cost per unit.
• Look for advertised sales in the newspaper or in the store's windows and aisles.
• Reduce your need for paper towels and napkins by using cloth towels. The average family throws away about $300 a year in disposable towels.
• Buy paper products at dollar stores.
• Use toilet paper instead of facial tissue.
• Use plastic grocery bags instead of costly trash bags when possible.
• Buy non-perishable products in bulk during sales.
• Buy generic brands.
• Bake bread, cakes, and pastries rather than buying packaged or store-prepared items.
• Have your butcher cut lean meats for you instead of purchasing pre-packaged meats.
• Substitute turkey meats, which are lower in cost and cholesterol, for beef.
• Buy whole chickens and cut them yourself instead of buying specific parts.
• Eliminate unhealthy snacks.
• Total your basket of items before you check out to see if you are within your budget.
• Items such as candy and magazines displayed near the checkout lane are there to tempt you into buying. Use this knowledge to avoid temptation and stick to your list.
• Check your receipt to make sure that you were properly charged.

*Tactic 12b Grow Your Own Food*

It can be fun and rewarding to get your hands dirty planting seeds that will grow to bear fruits and vegetables. Not only will you save on your grocery bill but you will enjoy a diet of fresh, homegrown produce. Being a gardener will give you pride in your green thumb and extra spending money from your savings when you stop buying produce in stores. For support and direction, there are several books, magazines, web sites, and weekly television shows that offer tips on how to tend your garden. In addition to feeding your family, extra produce could be sold at a local farmers market.

*Tactic 12c The Three Rs: Repeat, Reuse, and Replenish*

- *Repeat*—A cost- and health-saving alternative to fast food is to bring leftovers for lunch.
- *Reuse*—Reduce your coffee-making expenses by mixing old grounds with fresh. The ratio is four portions of old to one portion of new. For health reasons, do not use grounds that are more than one hour old.
- *Replenish*—Fill empty water bottles with filtered tap water or from large water bottles that allow you to purchase in bulk quantities.

*Tactic 12d Eat Out for Less*

These are great ways to save money when eating out:

- *Use Special Offer Coupons*—Many restaurants offer coupons in the newspaper or in coupon booklets. Usually, the discount is the value of the least expensive of two entrees, including the removal of that item's sales tax. However, your tip should be based on the full price of your meal, disregarding the discount.
- *Choose Coffee Alternatives*—Instead of buying your on-the-go coffee at an expensive chain get it from a gasoline or convenience store or fast-food outlet at a fraction of the cost.
- *Eat at Self-Serve Restaurants or Cafeterias*—This style of restaurant removes the cost of tip. Also, these eateries usually have lower overall expenses, which cuts the cost of food for you.
- *Eat Out for Lunch or Early Dinner*—Many restaurants offer weekday lunch specials to induce the business crowd. In addition, many restaurants offer early dinner specials to increase activity during the slow hours, usually from 5 to 6 P.M.

**Solution 13: Turn Your Hobby into Cash**

This is a fun way to increase your income by doing the things you like to do. Some of the more profitable hobbies are woodworking, painting, needlepoint, sewing, cooking, baking, and various crafts. In addition to community fairs and craft shows, the internet has sites to help promote your creations.

**Solution 14: Do-It-Yourself Repairs and Maintenance**

• *Home and Vehicle*—The savings earned by doing your own home and vehicle repairs and maintenance can be immense. You can take advantage of do-it-yourself practical knowledge in numerous books, websites, magazines, TV programs, and videos, which may save you thousands in labor costs alone.

• *Hair Care*—You should consider cutting your own hair and the hair of your family members. This could save an average family more than $500 each year.

• *Lawn Care*—In addition to saving hundreds of dollars on something you can do yourself, you can burn a lot of calories when cutting your grass. Thus, you can save on lawn care and a health club membership.

**Solution 15: Organize a Garage Sale**

The junk stored in your attic, garage, and basement may be considered a treasure by someone else. You should sift through your belongings to determine what to keep, what to sell, and what to give to charitable organizations. Donations to charities are tax deductible. Make an effort to get rid of things without sentimental value that you won't use again.

Tips for a Successful Yard Sale:

• Identify items for sale by searching your closet, attic, garage, basement, bookcases, and under your beds.

• Research community guidelines, permits, and restrictions that may apply.

• A minimum of two workers are needed —a cashier and a salesperson.

• Select a weekend date that does not conflict with other community activities.

• Advertise with neighborhood signs and in the local newspaper.

- Prepare items for display the day before.
- Create a positive atmosphere with upbeat music, plants, and balloons.
- Package similar inexpensive items together as one unit.
- Label items with their starting price.
- Have lots of small bills and coins for change.
- Stimulate conversation with bargain hunters.
- Negotiate, and remember that your goal is to sell everything.

**Solution 16: Bid on Seized or Repossessed Property at Auctions**

Property seized by the police, the IRS, and other federal agencies along with property repossessed by banks and lending institutions can be purchased for a fraction of the actual value. Items include homes, buildings, vacant land, vehicles, jewelry, clothing, computers, televisions, stereos, and much more.

Due to the poor economy and layoffs, the repossession of homes and vehicles is at an all-time high. As a result, you can find a large variety of homes, ranging from shacks to mansions, and vehicles, ranging from clunkers to racecars. The condition of these items varies from slightly used to trashed, but you can find a few gems. The majority are in good condition. According to EzineArticles.com, "It is not uncommon to purchase a vehicle at 80-90% off its retail value."

CHAPTER 3

# Reorganize Existing Debt

Financial freedom means unlocking the chains of debt that constrain our joy and independence. The word "debt" comes from the Latin word *debere,* which means to owe. Unnecessary debt is the number one cause of many personal financial problems. It is also the reason for most of our country's economic problems.

However, all debt is not bad. In fact, *controlled debt* is a necessity in today's society. Thus, it is important to distinguish between controlled debt and *unnecessary debt.* I use the term unnecessary debt to distinguish it from our normal monthly expenses (controlled debt) such as utility bills, mortgages, car payments, and insurance payments.

Unnecessary debt is excessive amounts owed to creditors for the purchasing of unessential and extravagant items. Unnecessary debt takes away your financial freedom. It makes you a prisoner to your creditors. The third building block strategy helps release you from this bondage by reorganizing existing debt.

**Solution 17: Pay Your Bills on Time**

Don't procrastinate or neglect paying your monthly obligations. Any delay costs money. Regardless of other obligations of time and money, it is your first responsibility to repay your creditors in a timely manner. Prompt payment avoids costly late fees and interest penalties and improves your credit score (see Solution 7, page 21).

**Solution 18: Repay Existing Debt with Accelerated Payments**

The first step in reorganizing debt is to make a list of all of your loan balances with their corresponding interest rates. You should focus on repaying the highest-interest debt as fast as possible.

This means increasing your monthly payments above the minimum requirement. Accelerated payments drastically reduce the interest paid on a loan by eliminating several months of payment. In fact, by increasing your monthly payment by four percent, you could reduce the length of time required to pay off the loan by more than 80 percent as seen in the example found in Solution 5 on page 19.

In order to find the money to rapidly pay off your loans, you should use some of the income saved with the strategies found in Strategy 2.

### Solution 19: Renegotiate Existing Loan Conditions

A simple phone call to your lender could save you lots of money. Some lenders and credit card companies may allow you to reduce or eliminate late charges, renegotiate interest rates, or even reduce your balance. This settlement can be arranged with a lump sum payment or fixed monthly payments, lowering the current balance by as much as 50 percent. In some cases, it may be even more. Terms vary with each creditor. Depending on the amount of the adjustment, it may be considered taxable income and the creditor may send you a 1099 tax form accordingly. A reorganization may also affect your credit rating. Discuss all options and consequences with the lender. Be sure to get the settlement terms in writing from the creditor.

### Solution 20: Consider Refinancing Your Mortgage

*Tactic 20a Know when to Refinance*

Refinancing existing home mortgages to take advantage of lower mortgage rates can drastically reduce the monthly payments of homeowners. In fact, the average homeowner can reduce their monthly principal and interest (P&I) payment by as much as 20 percent as a result of only a two to three percent drop in the annual interest rate. However, since there are many factors involved in determining if refinancing is beneficial, you should not make this decision hastily.

You should first consider five questions:

1. How Long do You Plan to Own Your Current Home?

If you plan to sell your home in less than three years, your monthly mortgage (P&I) reduction will probably not offset the upfront closing cost of refinancing.

2. How Much of a Drop in Interest Rate Justifies Refinancing?

Generally, if you plan to live in your home for more than three years, a two percent drop in the annual percentage rate of your original mortgage justifies refinancing. These conditions allow you to recoup the closing costs, which include such items as points, appraisal fees, inspections fees, title insurance, etc.

3. Would Your New Mortgage Increase Your Total Payment?

Don't be misled by the immediate monthly cash flow resulting from a new mortgage with lower interest rates. If the new mortgage extends the term of your loan, this plan may not be a long-term solution since your accumulated interest may be drastically increased.

4. Does Your Current Mortgage Contain Prepayment Penalties?

Some older mortgages contained penalty clauses that applied to early full repayment of the loan, usually within the first five years. Although these penalties are seldom part of new mortgages, you should make certain your loan does not contain a penalty.

5. How Will the Lower Interest Affect Your Taxes?

Due to resultant lower paid interest, your tax deduction is reduced. This affects your net gain.

In addition to these questions, you should be aware that refinancing is typically not an automatic process. Often you must re-qualify for the new loan even if you use the same mortgage company.

Once you determine that refinancing is a wise option, ask your current lender to modify or renegotiate your current loan instead of setting up a completely new mortgage. This reorganization could save you money and hassle. However, if your mortgagor requires a new loan, you should see if your lender will provide you with special treatment. This preferential service may include reducing your discount points and/or eliminating your origination fees.

*Tactic 20b Investigate Mortgage Options*

As you consider the option of refinancing or buying a new home, you should investigate what mortgage term best fits your needs. The two most common terms are the 30-year and the 15-year fixed mortgages. Fixed means your rate will not change during the term of the loan. The 15-year mortgage usually has a slightly lower interest rate than the 30-year mortgage. However, you should consider all of the facts when considering which option is best for you.

The chart below compares the two types of mortgages. The categories of Interest Savings and Monthly Difference in P&I Payment are meant to represent a comparison of the mortgage types.

| | 30-Year Mortgage | 15-Year Mortgage |
|---|---|---|
| Principal | $100,000.00 | $100,000.00 |
| Interest Rate | 6.00% | 5.68% |
| Monthly P&I | $599.95 | $826.67 |
| Payout | $215,982.00 | $148,800.60 |
| Interest | $115,982.00 | $48,800.60 |
| Interest Savings (Gross) | | $67,181.40 |
| Net Interest Savings After Taxes (Based on a 15% Tax Bracket) | | $57,104.19 |
| Monthly Difference in P&I Payment | $226.72 | |

According to the 15-year model, by increasing your monthly P&I $226.72 you will eliminate half of your payments. This would save you $67,181.40 in unpaid interest. Since mortgage interest payments are usually tax deductible, these savings are eligible for taxation. Thus, your savings after taxes are reduced to $57,104.19, based on a 15 percent tax bracket.

Another option when using the 30-year mortgage is to use your monthly savings to pay off high credit card balances.

Before making a decision on your mortgage term, consider your unique conditions, including tax impact. In most cases, it is best to select the 30-year mortgage without a pre-penalty clause. This gives you the flexibility to choose how to use the monthly savings on your payment. You have the freedom to pay any additional amount toward your principal at anytime and are not tied to a higher monthly payment that may become difficult to maintain.

**Solution 21: Wisely Consolidate Debt**

One way to overcome your debt is to reorganize and consolidate all of your many credit balances into one convenient loan with a lower interest rate.

Two Alternatives for Debt Consolidation:

1. Refinance your existing debt into a home equity loan. This can often reduce your many monthly payments into one smaller, more affordable payment. The interest may also be tax deductible.
2. Add the amount of your combined debt to the amount you seek to borrow when refinancing your mortgage. As with the home equity loan, the interest may be tax deductible in many circumstances.

A word of caution, when you consolidate with an equity loan or refinancing your existing mortgage, your house is collateral. Thus, if you don't pay the monthly note, your house can be seized by the mortgage company. Also, do not get back into financial trouble by using credit cards irresponsibly (see Solution 5, page 19).

However, no matter what type of loan you use to reorganize your existing debt, don't let the smaller payment fool you.

There are several factors to consider:

- Current balance for existing debt.
- Interest rate for existing debt.
- Current monthly payment compared to consolidated payment.
- Tax advantage of consolidation loan.
- Use of monthly savings.

*Example:* Marge and Bobby were tired of paying several high-interest loans that totaled $473.86 per month. Thus, the couple decided to refinance all of their existing debt into a home equity loan with a low interest rate.

| Loan | Remaining Months | Monthly Payment | Balance | Total Payout | Interest Rate |
|---|---|---|---|---|---|
| A | 12 | $99.85 | $1,089.09 | $1,198.20 | 18% |
| B | 3 | $189.12 | $545.40 | $567.36 | 24% |
| C | 6 | $184.89 | $1,048.57 | $1,109.34 | 19.6% |
| **Total** | | **$473.86** | **$2,683.06** | **$2,874.90** | |

When the $2,683.06 balance is refinanced at 6.25 percent for five years, the monthly payment is $52.18 (final payment is $52.46) with a total payout of $3,131.08. This payout is $256.18 more than the prior payout for the combined loans. As you can see, even though this new loan temporarily reduces your monthly payment, the overall debt is increased despite the lower interest rate and tax savings.

CHAPTER 4

# Maximize Insurance While Minimizing Cost

*Note:* Since the process of selecting insurance coverage is very complicated, this planning should be conducted with the support of experienced professionals. The mission of this strategy is to give an overview of various insurance topics, not to offer specific advice.

The purpose of insurance is to set aside a reserve fund as a means of risk management. As a good manager of your assets, it is important to properly protect yourself, your family, and your possessions from injury or damage which would result in financial hemorrhage. Insurance is not intended to take away all chance of or culpability for risk but to provide protection and indemnification in the event of a fiscally devastating occurrence. This is why many policies provide deductible or waiting period options. In addition to economic loss caused by sickness, injury, disability, or death you need indemnification for personal liability suits as well as protection for your property.

*Insurance*—"A fund that is established and designed for the purpose of providing protection against a substantial risk, loss, harm or ruin. It is defined by a contract (terms of fund disbursement and conditions) in which an insurer or underwriter (director of fund) indemnifies or guarantees to pay a sum of money to a policyholder (fund participant who pays a premium to the fund) in the event of a loss as stated in the contract."

A carefully planned insurance program, which adequately offers the protection you need at a reasonable price, is a necessity. The fourth building block strategy helps you lower your premiums, prevent gaps in coverage, and eliminate duplicate (and therefore unnecessary) insurance. It also keeps you from being over- or under-insured.

These seven fundamental tactics ensure that you get the best protection for your premium:

1. *Choose Reputable Agents and Carriers*—It is important to check the reputation of your agent(s) and carrier(s) for stability, professionalism, and integrity.
2. *Learn the Basics*—As a prudent customer, it is critical to learn the basic coverage, exclusions, limitations, and conditions of your policies.
3. *Check the Premium*—Since the rating process of most insurance policies is very complicated, it is important that you and your agent review the final agreement for clarity. This includes verification of all classifications, applicable discounts, and the premium.
4. *Use Options Wisely*—Get rid of unnecessary coverage that is costing you money.
5. *Choose Cost-Effective Deductible(s)*—When getting a quote, you should ask to look at several deductible options to make sure which alternative best fits your economic needs.
6. *Shop for a Competitive Premium*—Before making a policy decision, a judicious insurance purchaser obtains at least three written quotes from more than one insurance company.
7. *Stay Claim-Free*—A small claim may cause your carrier to surcharge your policy in the future or cancel your coverage. You should always be aware of how claims affects your premium in the long run.

**Solution 22: Choose a Great Agent / Financial Advisor**

Insurance is a complex investment that requires the advice of someone trustworthy. Don't be confused by self-proclaimed insurance experts.

When selecting an agent, use the following process:

1. Investigate the integrity of your prospective counselor by contacting your state's insurance commissioner (Licensing Division) and the Better Business Bureau.
2. Ask for a letter of reference from at least three clients of the potential advisor.

3. Make sure he has your interest as his top priority, not his own personal gain.
4. Ensure that your counselor is knowledgeable about the insurance plans you need. Verify certifications, designations, and credentials. Here are some of the major designations:

Property and Casualty Advisors:

CIC: Certified Insurance Counselors
CPCU: Certified Property and Casualty Underwriter
CPIW: Certified Professional Insurance Women

Financial Services Advisors

CFP: Certified Financial Planner
ChFC: Chartered Financial Consultant
CLU: Chartered Life Underwriter
CPA: Certified Public Account
LUTCF: Life Underwriting Training Counsel Fellow

**Solution 23: Choose a Stable Carrier**

Before buying any form of insurance, verify that the carrier is rated as superior or excellent by at least two of the leading companies that evaluate the stability and performance of insurers. Next, determine if the company has been admitted to legally do business in your state. If it hasn't, then your policy will not be protected by your state's Guarantee Fund. The Guarantee Fund pays all or part of claims if an admitted carrier becomes insolvent. In other words, if your insurance company is bankrupt or otherwise unable to fulfill its financial obligation to you. Finally, contact the Better Business Bureau and the Commissioner of Insurance in your state to discover if any complaints have been filed against the insurer.

**Solution 24: Maximize Your Homeowners Insurance**

*Homeowners insurance,* which is sometimes called hazard insurance, basically protects the policyholder from various types of loss resulting from home ownership.

Coverage includes:

- *Property*—coverage for your home, possessions, adjacent structures, and loss of use or additional living expenses (ALE) with certain exclusions
- *Liability*—coverage for third-party claims that arise from accidents that may occur at home.

The primary exclusions include flood, earthquake, nuclear explosion, "Acts of God," and war. Coastal areas may have a windstorm exclusion.

*Tactic 24a Learn the Basics: Avoid Being Over- or Under-Insured*

Home insurance is based on the value of your home. The higher your home's value, the higher your premium and, therefore, your coverage in the event of an accident. If your house is over-insured, you are throwing money away by paying an excessively high premium. On the other hand, if your dwelling is under-insured and you suffer a loss you may be severely penalized by a co-insurance clause. This provision if it is in your policy, states that you must insure your dwelling for the proper value.

Since most carriers annually increase your dwelling limits based on a formula, it is possible your current dwelling value is not your actual value. Insurance companies conduct valuations based on construction indexes for various geographical territories. This increase is automatically added to the value of your home on the declaration of coverage page of your homeowners. It does not take into consideration market values. Thus, after a few years, the value of your home on the policy may be off. This is a good reason to update your policy annually.

*Tactic 24b Check the Premium: Take Advantage of Credits*

Most insurance carriers offer premium credits for various conditions. Make sure your agent has applied all the credits you earn.

Possible Credits:

- Burglar alarms (Local or central station)
- Fire alarms (Local or central station)

- Smoke alarms
- Dead-bolt locks
- Being loss-free for three years
- New home

*Tactic 24c Use Options Wisely: Choose Replacement Cost*

Property replacement coverage is provided on either an *actual cash value* (ACV) basis or a *guaranteed replacement cost* (GRC) basis. ACV coverage only pays the cost to replace your damaged property, less the property's depreciation due to age and wear.

On the other hand, GRC coverage reimburses the policyholder for the actual cost to replace the item(s) damaged or destroyed. However, insurers only pay GRC when you replace the item with one of equivalent type and value. Otherwise, you will be paid the ACV for the item.

*Tactic 24d Use Options Wisely: Select the Essentials*

Important coverage options available for property policies include the scheduling of valuables such as jewelry, furs, guns, artwork, coins, collectables, musical instruments, antiques, and computer protection. (Scheduling means specifically adding to your policy items such as jewelry or musical instruments to a schedule. It lists the items with a description along with an agreed value of insurance.) Your insurance agent will assist you with selecting options to fit your specific needs and budget.

*Tactic 24e Choose Cost-Effective Deductibles*

Since insurance is only intended to provide coverage for a catastrophic loss, a prudent homeowner must take advantage of reasonable deductibles that substantially reduce the policy premium. Ask your agent to offer quotes for $500, $1,000, and $2,500 deductibles.

*Note:* In coastal areas, a windstorm/hail deductible or hurricane deductible applies along with the standard deductible for all other coverage. This is usually a percentage of the value of the home ranging from 2 to 5 percent.

*Tactic 24f Shop for a Competitive Premium*

Since most renewal premiums are paid by your mortgage company via your escrow account (the money set aside by your mortgagor for property taxes, renewal premiums, and mortgage insurance), it is easy for you, the policyholder, to forget to obtain renewal quotes for your policy. Insurance agents automatically send you and your mortgage company the renewal policy, along with an invoice to your mortgage company, 60 days prior to the renewal date.

You must take the initiative to obtain at least two other alternative quotes 75 days prior to the renewal date. At that time, you must inform your mortgage company not to automatically pay the renewal invoice since you are considering alternate quotes. However, don't forget to inform your mortgage company of your renewal decision. The *Easy Insurance Summary* on page 64 will help you organize the quotation process.

*Tactic 24g Stay Claim-Free: Don't Make Small Claims*

The underwriting guidelines of major insurance carriers are becoming more restrictive as their loss ratio increases. As a result, underwriters will cancel policyholders who have reported multiple claims during a three year period. This is another reason to choose a higher deductible.

**Solution 25: Maximize Your Vehicle Insurance**

*Auto Insurance* premiums are rapidly increasing each year even though the value of your liability limit is decreasing due to inflation. Before we offer tactics to maximize coverage and save money, you need a better understanding of the risks and coverage forms.

The Four Types of Risk:

*1. Death, Injury, and Disability of Yourself or an Immediate Family Member*—In addition to medical and possible funeral expenses, you and your family may also suffer a loss of income due to injuries resulting from an automobile accident.
*2. Third-Party Claims*—If found to be legally at fault in an accident you are financially responsible for the pain and suffering, bodily injuries (including medical and rehabilitation costs), and/or

deaths of your passengers (other than family members) and/or third parties. Additionally, you are monetarily obligated to repair or replace the property of others that you damaged or destroyed.
3. *Damage to or Loss of Your Vehicle*—In the event of an accident involving your vehicle, you will be reimbursed for the collision damage (less the deductible). Your vehicle may be damaged by fire, hail, windstorm, smoke, falling objects, or other peril. It may even be stolen. This coverage also pays for damage resulting from accidents caused by uninsured or underinsured motorists.
4. *Loss of Use*—This includes the rental cost incurred for a temporary replacement.

The Four Parts of Auto Coverage:

PART A: LIABILITY COVERAGE
PART B: MEDICAL PAYMENTS
PART C: UNINSURED/UNDER-INSURED MOTORISTS
PART D: PHYSICAL DAMAGE

*Liability coverage* obligates the insurer to pay any claims as described in Risk 2 which result from an accident in which the policyholder is legally at fault on behalf of the insured. Most carriers offer protection for bodily injury and property damage as one combined single limit (CSL), but some offer split limits as an option. Under CSL, the carrier provides one aggregate limit for both the total bodily injury costs and property damage losses of a single occurrence. In contrast, split limits allow you to choose a bodily injury limit per potential person involved and its corresponding per accident aggregate, along with a separate limit for property damage.

It is important to point out that with most insurers, the carrier's defense costs, including claim handling and investigation, are not charged against your liability limit.

*Example:* If the policy limits shown on the declaration page of your contract is $100,000 CSL, your carrier will indemnify you for a total of $100,000 for all incurred bodily injuries and property damage losses per accident.

On the other hand, if your policy limits show split limits of $50,000/$100,000/$50,000, your contract will pay $50,000 per person for bodily injuries, with an aggregate of $100,000 per loss. Any resulting property damage claim for a given accident will be paid up to $50,000. Although the combined total of the bodily injury and property damage aggregates of split limits is greater than the CSL equivalent, the bodily injury limit per person is only half that of the CSL protection.

*Medical payments coverage* obligates your carrier to pay or reimburse you, the policyholder, for medical expenses (and funeral services) that are incurred by the insured and/or passengers injured while in a covered vehicle. The basic limit for this coverage is $1,000 per person, but it can be increased for an additional premium. There is no aggregate per accident. If you have adequate health coverage and a prearranged funeral plan, this protection may be unnecessary.

*Uninsured / under-insured motorist (UM) coverage* enables the policyholder to make a claim or sue his own carrier for bodily or personal injury damages arising from an incident caused by an uninsured or under-insured motorist, a hit-and-run driver, or an at-fault driver whose insurance carrier becomes insolvent. In recent years, the premium for this important coverage has drastically increased due to the increasing number of inadequately insured motorists and insolvent companies. Since this coverage is no longer inexpensive, it is necessary for you and your advisor to choose a sufficient but reasonable limit. Remember that your UM limit does not have to be equal to your other automobile liability limits. However, you may be required by state law to sign a form stating that you reject or reduce this limit.

*Physical Damage:*

- *Collision coverage* reimburses the policyholder for damage or total loss resulting from the insured vehicle's collision with another object or vehicle. This coverage, which offers several deductible options, may respond in both at-fault and non-at-fault situations. If a third party is at-fault but does not have insurance, then the collision coverage (less the deductible) is paid by your company. Your insurance carrier is then responsible to bring action against the negligent party for their loss and the insured's deductible.

• *Comprehensive coverage, otherwise known as loss other than collision,* is considered to be a loss caused by any of the following:

- Missiles or falling objects;
- Fire;
- Theft or larceny;
- Explosion or earthquake;
- Windstorm;
- Hail, water, or flood;
- Malicious mischief or vandalism;
- Riot or civil commotion

*Rental reimbursement coverage* pays the insured to rent a substitute vehicle while the covered automobile is disabled due to an insured loss. The coverage is limited to a specific amount per day with a 30-day aggregate limitation.

*Tactic 25a Learn the Basics: Select the Right Liability Limits*

Your minimum CSL or bodily injury split limits aggregate should be at least equal to three times your *net worth*.

In other words, if your net worth is $100,000, multiply this amount by three, which results in a $300,000 potential exposure to third party claims. Therefore, you should choose $300,000 CSL or at least $100,000/$300,000/$100,000 split limits as your minimum liability protection. Your property damage aggregate should be at least equal to your bodily injury per person limit.

The CSL limits available for your automobile's underlying coverage are:

$ 30,000 CSL
50,000 CSL
100,000 CSL
300,000 CSL
500,000 CSL
1,000,000 CSL (available through only a few carriers)

The most common split limits available for your automobile underlying coverage are:

| BODILY INJURY | PROPERTY DAMAGE |
|---|---|
| $10,000 per person / $20,000 aggregate | $10,000 aggregate |
| 25,000 per person / 50,000 aggregate | 25,000 aggregate |
| 50,000 per person / 100,000 aggregate | 50,000 aggregate |
| 100,000 per person / 300,000 aggregate | 100,000 aggregate |
| 250,000 per person / 500,000 aggregate | 100,000 aggregate |

Although split limits coverage reduces your bodily injury limit per person, it does increase the total bodily injury and property damage aggregate limits per accident while substantially decreasing your total premium.

*Tactic 25b Learn the Basics: Select the Right Uninsured Motorist Limit*

One way to establish your appropriate UM limit is to determine your anticipated financial needs if you were to become injured or disabled due to an accident.

You should consider these three factors:

1. Most of your medical bills would be paid by your health insurance or workers compensation coverage.
2. Your lifestyle would be different.
3. Economical Uninsured Motorists may be an affordable option if it is available through your insurance carrier. (This coverage pays only for incurred loss such as medical bills, lost wages, etc. It does not include pain and suffering. Therefore, this coverage is a lot less expensive.)

*Tactic 25c Check the Premium: Verify Classifications*

The cost of your automobile insurance premium is determined by rating factors based on your various drivers' individual classifications. It is important for you to understand this classification process since a mistake could cost you hundreds of dollars.

Basic Classifications:

- *Vehicle Use*—Classifications range from the highest rate for business use to the lowest rate for limited personal use.
- *Multi-Car Discounts*—A 20 percent discount is applied to all coverage (except uninsured/underinsured motorist, towing and labor, and medical payments) for all cars owned and operated by the insured under a single master policy.
- *Driver Age*—The age of drivers affects their vehicle premium. Basically, young drivers (especially males) are drastically surcharged while mature drivers receive a discount.

*Tactic 25d Check the Premium: Young Driver Solutions*

The cost of insurance for young drivers is expensive, but there are ways that this premium may be reduced.

- *Driver's Education Credit*—Carriers offer a discount for young drivers who successfully complete a state-certified driver's education class. A certificate of completion is necessary.
- *Good Student Credit*—A high school or full-time college student who maintains a certain grade point average qualifies for this discount. A signed form of certification must be completed by the educational institution on a yearly basis.
- *Incidental Driver Classification*—The premium for a young part-time driver is much less than if they are listed as a primary driver of a specific vehicle.
- *Student Away at School*—If a full-time student lives more than 100 miles from the family residence, many carriers apply a discount to the normal young driver rates.

*Tactic 25e Check the Premium: Take Advantage of Credits*

When shopping automobile insurance premiums, you must inform your agent of any of the following discounts that may apply to your vehicles. Discounts vary by state and carrier.

Types of Discounts:

- Multi-car
- Anti-theft device
- Passive restraints (air bag and/or automatic seat belts)
- Anti-lock brakes

- Senior citizen
- Driver training for young drivers (state certified)
- Good student for young drivers
- Loss-free
- Low mileage
- Multi-policy package
- Non-smoking
- Adult defensive driving course
- Carpool

*Tactic 25f Use Options Wisely: Modify Coverage to Fit Needs*

The following coverage parts may not be worth the premium for the small potential risk:

• *Medical Payments*—Since a large part of your medical expenses resulting from an vehicle accident should be covered by your health insurance or, in some cases, workers' compensation, this option reimburses you for your deductible and co-insurance payments.
• *Comprehensive and Collision Coverage for Low-Value and/or Old Vehicles*—In the event of a small loss, if your car is valued under $1,500 and/or is over six model years old, your repair bill may exceed the value of your car. In this situation, your claim adjuster will probably declare the vehicle a total loss and will offer you only a small amount to replace it. In most cases, a prudent policyholder removes this coverage and saves on premium reductions. In order to determine if you should keep this protection, compare the physical damage premiums with an anticipated claim payment in the event of a total or partial loss. If your rate of return is not good, do not invest in physical damage coverage.

*Tactic 25g Choose Cost-Effective Deductibles*

Since the premium for your physical damage coverage is based on many factors, such as driver and use classifications along with model and age of vehicle, you should request quotations for all available deductible options. In one situation when acting as an agent I quoted the policyholder over a $300 annual savings to increase their deductible from $250 to $500. The thing to remember is to compare your premium reduction with your increase in deductible amount. Then decide if this makes financial sense.

*Tactic 25h Shop for a Competitive Premium*

As stated earlier, good insurance purchasers must take the initiative to review their premium at least once a year. Since most agents send renewal policies without contacting their clients for updates, the chances of a rating error in the company's favor is highly possible.

The pricing of insurance companies varies greatly from year to year. The current most competitive carrier may have been the least competitive three years ago. On the other hand, your present carrier may drastically increase their rates by as much as 20 percent in a year. A study of one market area shows premiums quoted by the major national carriers varying by as much as 50 percent.

Also, when shopping premiums you should determine if a package deal with the same carrier providing both your homeowners and auto coverage would save money. Some insurers offer substantial discounts for joint policies, which also helps you by preventing potential gaps and coverage duplication.

By examining new options at every renewal period (at least 30 days prior to the renewal date) you will motivate your current agent to go the extra mile finding the best coverage at the most competitive prices. The *Easy Insurance Summary* on page 64 will help you with the quotation process.

*Tactic 25i Stay Claim-Free: Keep a Clean Driving Record*

The only way you can control the pricing of your insurance is by keeping an accident-free driving record with no moving violations. If you are a cautious driver, you will be rewarded with competitive rates.

*The At-Fault Accident Surcharge*—When a listed driver on a policy has an at-fault accident, his premium usually rises based on a claim surcharge.

*The Cancellation of Your Policy Due to Frequent Claims*—The underwriting guidelines of major insurance carriers are becoming more restrictive as their loss ratio increases. As a result, insurers will cancel policies where the insured has reported multiple collision (and sometimes comprehensive) claims during a three year period. This cancellation forces you to seek higher-priced carriers or the Assigned Risk Plan as alternative insurance. Insurers sell Assigned Risk plans to high-risk drivers at a very high rate based on the likelihood of a claim against the insured.

*Check With Your Agent or Advisor*—Before reporting a small claim to your carrier, ask your agent to determine how this loss will affect your premium.

**Solution 26: Maximize Your Health Insurance**

The skyrocketing cost of health care is a critical concern of most hardworking Americans. The severity of this problem has forced many U.S. citizens to discontinue their unaffordable health insurance, while some unhealthy Americans are unable to secure coverage at all. According to statistics, the average annual cost of family health insurance in the United States represents more than 12 percent of their total income.

Several solutions to this crucial issue are currently under debate in various government committees. However, no immediate answer to stop or control this dilemma has been found. While this heated debate continues, it is up to each individual or employer to choose the best health care protection among the plans currently available.

This decision has been made even more difficult due to the recent insolvency of carriers, a tightening of benefits and the rapidly rising cost of health care. Therefore, before you make a decision, you should learn the basics of the two major forms of health insurance programs.

Two Major Health Insurance Policies:

- *Fee-for-Service* and
- *Managed Care*
  - HMO (Health Maintenance Organization)
  - POS (Point of Service)
  - PPO (Preferred Provider Organization)

*Fee-for-Service*

The most popular medical policy is the traditional Fee-for-Service plan, which pays for health services as needed per the conditions of the policy. This coverage is designed to indemnify the insured against loss due to illness or accidental injury.

Under this type of plan, the insurer pays medical bills resulting from a covered claim once the annual deductible has been surpassed. After the deductible, the next layer of medical expenses (normally $5,000 total) is paid on a contribution basis otherwise known as co-insurance. Usually a carrier pays up to 80 percent of these charges while the insured pays the other 20 percent. Therefore, your total policy deductible and co-insurance payment make up what is commonly referred to as your out-of-pocket expense. The carrier pays any qualified charge exceeding the out-of-pocket deductible in full up to the policy's maximum limit.

The best feature of the traditional plan is that the insured has the right to seek medical services from any physician, hospital, or health provider they choose (non-traditional fee-for-service plans require the insured to use a provider network). However, it does have its drawbacks.

Freedom of choice usually makes fee-for-service plans more expensive than alternative programs once you add in your out-of-pocket expenses. In addition, as a safeguard against claim abuse the carrier reviews all submitted medical bills to determine if they are "reasonable and customary." This phrase means the carrier compares your expenses to prior medical fees in your community. In lieu of this review your coverage may be contingent on fee limits. An insured person with this form of policy should be aware that their carrier has the right not to pay charges they deem unnecessary or excessive. Also, many policies require pre-certification of health services. Before undergoing any medical procedure, your physician should contact your health insurance carrier to determine if their services will be covered.

Positive Features:

- Complete freedom to select physicians and specialists
- Emergency coverage available throughout the U.S.

Negative Features:

- Usually more expensive than managed care plans once you add in deductibles and co-insurance payments

• The subjective qualifying criterion of "reasonable and customary"

*Managed Care: Health Maintenance Organization (HMO)*

The most popular managed care program is the Health Maintenance Organization (HMO). An HMO has a definite edge over traditional plans when it comes to added benefits and the way it handles deductibles and co-payments. Among the additional benefits are preventive care, immunizations, and well-baby visits. Plans often include payment for eyeglasses and prescription drugs.

Although this form of coverage offers its members more benefits for their premium than fee-for-service plans, it offers less flexibility in choosing your doctor and hospital, barring certain emergency situations. The foundation of a managed care program is the network of physicians and health care providers available to its members, but this often becomes a double-edged sword when policyholders are restricted to only these designated members. There is no certainty that a doctor will remain on the HMO's approved list and therefore no guarantee that you will be able to continue seeing your doctor. If your doctor is removed from the network the insured must choose a new physician from a list.

With regards to payment of medical expenses, for the most part there are no deductibles. Another feature allows members to pay only a small fee (co-pay) for an office visit. However, this policy may require a referral from your primary care physician before it will pay any specialists' charges. This requirement may delay your care as a result of coordinating the referral.

Before selecting an HMO plan, you should investigate it thoroughly since all HMO's are not alike.

HMO Checklist:

• Check the insurance provider's reputation and financial statement.
• Examine the list of participating physicians, looking for quality of care offered.
• Evaluate how well the plan meets your health needs.
• Make sure that the HMO offers emergency out of state coverage.

Positive Features:

- Small fee for office visits.
- No deductibles or co-insurance payments for network providers.
- Usually offers competent physicians and other health care providers.
- Less overall cost for protection.
- Additional benefits: Preventive care, well baby, etc.

Negative Features:

- You must choose among a limited network physicians and providers.
- Your primary care physician may be required to provide a referral for specialists, which may cause a delay in obtainment of care.

*Managed Care: Point of Service (POS)*

A POS is similar to an HMO but allows an insured to go outside the provider network. However, additional fees and co-insurance applies.

*Managed Care: Preferred Provider Organizations (PPO)*

This type of managed care plan is a variation on the HMO concept. In a PPO a selected group of independent hospitals and medical practitioners located in specific regional area agree to provide medical services at discounted or prearranged rates. Unlike most HMO's, the health providers are compensated on a fee-for-service basis instead of a flat monthly fee.

*Tactic 26a Learn the Basics: Use Pre-Tax Dollars for Medical Expenses*

Some employers offer payroll deduction programs, such as the Section 125 Plan (See Solution 31), that allow you to deduct part of your salary for certain qualified expenses on a pre-tax basis. If you participate in such a program you set aside money through payroll deductions for health insurance premiums and uninsured medical costs, which includes your out-of-pocket expenses. The deductions taken from your paycheck for insurance aren't taxed, meaning that you save all the money that would have gone to taxes in any other scenario. In this way you can save money while paying for insurance. These savings may amount to as much as 35 percent, depending on your tax bracket.

*Tactic 26b Learn the Basics: Consider Generic Drugs*

Generic drugs are less expensive than their brand-name counterparts even though both versions have identical active ingredients and meet U.S. Food and Drug Administration (FDA) standards for safety, purity, and effectiveness. According to the FDA, the reason for the price difference is that the manufacturers do not have the research and development costs of producing and marketing a new drug. Most insurance companies try to steer their policyholders toward generics by requiring higher co-pays for brand-name drugs. Ask your doctor about the generic alternatives to your drugs; you may save money on essentially the same product.

*Tactic 26c Choose Cost-Effective Deductibles or Co-Payments*

When searching for health insurance you must obtain several deductible, co-insurance, and co-payment options. This enables you to consider the overall effect of your premium when compared to your out-of-pocket expenses. Make sure you have a good understanding of how the deductible, co-insurance, and co-payments work when considering any plan. As stated earlier, the purpose of insurance is to prevent financial ruin. Always weigh the pros and cons of higher deductibles or co-payments, which defray the rapidly rising cost of health insurance but require more contribution from you in the event of an accident or illness.

*Tactic 26d Shop for a Competitive Premium*

Unlike other coverage, most health insurance is obtained through your employer as part of a group plan. However, no matter if you purchase medical insurance as an individual or through your employer, it is necessary to reevaluate your plan at least once a year. Therefore, before committing to any health policy you or your employer should do adequate research. Obtain at least three quotes from reputable and stable insurance carriers and/or managed health plans.

This checklist will assist you in your evaluation:

- List the benefits that are explicitly covered and those that are excluded.
- Determine the Maximum Lifetime Benefit. (The Maximum Lifetime Benefit is the total amount your carrier will pay during the entire period you are insured by that carrier.)
- Check the frequency of past rate increases and when the next increase is probable.
- Discover how pre-existing conditions are covered under the plan.
- Review all extra fees and limitations.
- Ask if pregnancy and mental illnesses or disorders (including alcohol and/or drug rehabilitation) are covered like any other sickness.

**Solution 27: Maximize Your Life Insurance**

The main reason to buy life insurance is to provide a sum of money to a beneficiary in the event of death. However, death benefit protection is no longer the sole purpose of life insurance. In fact, most of the presentations and illustrations currently presented by agents are designed to emphasize the tax deferred accumulation feature, which means your funds can grow with interest without paying taxes, instead of the lump sum benefit. Many life insurance salespeople present their products as retirement plans that offer life insurance as a bonus, while others promote them as tax deferred investment vehicles for specific goals such as college education. Any policy that provides a death benefit is a life insurance policy. On the other hand, if you need a structured savings plan which allows your investments to grow on a tax deferred basis, life insurance may be your best solution since it satisfies several needs. In order to decide which form of life insurance is best suited for you at this time, review the following summaries of the basic types of plans.

*Term insurance,* which offers the least expensive form of death protection, provides a stated benefit for a specific period with renewable options. The most common form of this policy is the Annual Renewal Term (ART), which is issued with a very inexpensive first-year premium that increases every year the contract remains in force. An alternative to the ART are the step rate or level term policies. Under this type, for a slightly higher initial premium, the insured may elect to pay a fixed rate for a specified period, such as five or 10 years. Regardless of form, term policies have no cash value.

As an added incentive to purchase permanent insurance, some renewable plans allow policyholders to convert their policy to permanent insurance without a medical examination.

If you only desire a death benefit until you retire, term insurance offers the least expensive way to obtain a lump sum death benefit. This form is helpful for people who have little cash to invest. Due to the small premium and low commission rate, many agents do not emphasize this product. Instead, they promote permanent contracts with higher commissions.

A *Whole Life* policy, unlike a term policy, provides an accumulated cash value that grows on a tax-deferred basis along with a standard death benefit. The premium is fixed for the life of the contract. This policy has three important features concerning the cash build up.

- *Paid-Up Premiums*—At some point during the contract term the insured may elect to discontinue premium payments while maintaining the same protection.
- *Low-Interest, Tax-Free Loans*—Policyholders are allowed to borrow funds at a low interest rate from their accumulated cash value. Since this is a loan, the amount borrowed is not subject to tax.
- *Surrender Value*—If the insured decides to cancel his or her policy, the surrender value of the accumulated funds is paid to the policyholder. However, the surrender value may reflect penalties that reduce the actual cash value.

A Whole Life policy is best suited for people who need protection beyond retirement and who also want to save for a specific long-term goal.

*Universal Life* adds the flexibility of increasing tax-deferred savings to the Whole Life concept. In this form, the insured pays a certain minimum premium for the death benefit and may pay extra into the cash accumulation fund. The resulting cash value will fluctuate depending on current interest rates and actual paid premiums. Universal Life is for those who desire permanent death benefits and total flexibility with both their premiums and protection.

*Variable Life* unites investment opportunities with insurance protection. Unlike Universal Life, this policy affords the opportunity to increase cash values and death benefits through good investment results. Policyholders have the choice of a variety of fixed income or variable rate options. Variable Life is best suited for those who desire to maximize their use of permanent insurance as a tax-deferred investment.

*Tactic 27a Learn the Basics: Decide Between Term and Permanent Insurance*

The type of insurance you purchase depends on your individual goals, needs, financial expertise, available funds, and determination. Keep in mind that most life insurance policies now offer tax-deferred savings as part of their contract.

Generally, term insurance gives the most death benefit for the premium when the policy holder is relatively young. However, term becomes extremely expensive in later years. Therefore, this is not practical if you plan to increase or continue this level of protection after retirement.

On the other hand, permanent insurance, which costs more, has the advantage of a cash value build up. This investment feature allows your savings to grow on a tax-deferred basis. However, due to administrative cost and commissions, your cash value grows slowly in the early years. If you need funds for an emergency during this initial period the surrender charges drastically reduce the cash value. In this situation, you would be better off buying term insurance and investing the difference.

The choice between term insurance and permanent insurance is purely individual. It is a choice that changes as your financial position grows. However, at some point in life, permanent, paid-up life insurance that extends past retirement may become a necessity.

As you compare your options, keep in mind that carriers who have the lowest term premiums usually don't offer the best permanent products and the leading carriers of permanent life insurance

usually have the highest term rates. When comparing term to permanent you should make sure your advisor has provided you the most competitive carrier's product for each option.
The following general statements can help give you direction in making your final decision on what type of insurance is best for you.

SIX REASONS TO BUY TERM AND
INVEST THE DIFFERENCE

1. If your need for a death benefit will be reduced or eliminated at age 65, consider buying term and investing the cost difference in a tax-deferred investment plan.
2. If your main priorities involve short- or medium-term goals, such as education or buying a home, do not use life insurance as a funding plan.
3. If you have accumulated bills, it is better to buy term insurance and use the difference to pay off loans.
4. If your main objective is to establish a retirement fund, buy term and invest the difference in annuities, which are long-term savings/investment accounts that provide income at retirement (Tactic 35d).
5. If you are an astute investor.
6. If you are under 40 years of age, it is often best to buy term insurance and use the difference to pay off debt and build equity by paying additional principle payments on your home mortgage and contributing to investments.

THREE REASONS TO BUY PERMANENT INSURANCE

1. If you desire a permanent, paid up life insurance past retirement, the best option is to buy permanent insurance while in your early forties.
2. If you lack the determination to save for long-term goals.
3. If you need a flexible savings plan that allows your funds to grow on a tax-deferred basis.

When comparing term insurance with permanent insurance, keep in mind that some agents and planners may be motivated by high commissions to sell permanent insurance that may not fit your goals or needs. Don't lose focus of what is the best option for you. Make sure your agent is working in your best interest and not just for profit.

*Tactic 27b Learn the Basics: Select the Correct Death Benefit*

Life insurance is not intended to make your survivors wealthy. Nonetheless, few individuals have adequate death protection. The main reason for this deficiency is a lack of understanding on behalf of the insured of the future economic needs of his family after death. As a general rule, most advisors recommend your protection be at least five times your gross annual income.

*Tactic 27c Use Options Wisely*

Life insurance policies offer various types of options. In order to get the most coverage for your policy, here is an explanation of some of the most popular options.

Popular Life Insurance Options:

- *Accidental Death Benefit*—This option, which is also known as the "double indemnity rider," pays an additional death benefit, usually twice the regular protection, if the insured dies due to an accident.
- *Family Insurance Rider*—A small death benefit for your spouse or dependents can be added to your policy by this option. This protection is provided in the form of term insurance. The premium will increase and no cash value will accumulate. This rider can be useful in situations where a spouse and/or children need only small protection, as the maximum protection is usually $10,000.
- *Guaranteed Purchase Rider*—This rider guarantees the insured the ability to increase his death benefit without having to prove insurability. However, this option to increase protection is restricted by the amount and timeframe in which it can be exercised.
- *Waiver of Premium*—If the insured becomes disabled, usually for more than six months, this rider waives the premiums of your life insurance policy for the duration of your disability. The usually small premium for this option makes it worth consideration if you have inadequate long-term disability coverage.
- *Supplemental Monthly Income*—This option provides the insured with a stream of income in case of disability. However, since the limit is usually quite small for the premium, a specific disability policy is more advantageous.

**EZ INSURANCE SUMMARY**

**HOMEOWNER INSURANCE**

| | | | | | |
|---|---|---|---|---|---|
| Policy # | | Effective Dates | / / | to | / / |
| Insurance Carrier | | Annual Premium | $ | | |
| Agency | | Phone Number | | | |
| Agent | | Fax Number | | | |

| Coverage Type | Value | Notes: |
|---|---|---|
| • Dwelling | $ | |
| • Contents | $ | |
| • Adjacent Structures | $ | |
| • Personal Liability | $ CSL | |
| • Medical Payments | $ | |
| | Deductible | |
| • Standard | | |
| • Other* | | *Windstorm / Hail or Hurricane Deductible |

**AUTOMOBILE INSURANCE**

| | | | | |
|---|---|---|---|---|
| Policy # | | Effective Dates | / / | to / / |
| Insurance Carrier | | Annual Premium | $ | |
| Agency | | Phone Number | | |
| Agent | | Fax Number | | |

| Coverage Type | Value | Notes: |
|---|---|---|
| • Liability (CSL) or | $ | |
| • Liability (BI) | $ | |
| • Liability (PD) | $ | |
| • Liability (UM) | $ | |
| • Medical Payment | $ | |
| | Deductible | |
| • Comprehensive | | |
| • Collision | | |

CHAPTER 5

# Reduce Your Taxes

A major portion of our hard-earned income is paid to the government. Federal income tax represents our largest tax expense. Since the Internal Revenue Service (IRS) has established various deductions through tax codes, we can reduce the amount of taxes we owe the government through careful planning. If we don't utilize these legal tax strategies, we are voluntarily paying the government more taxes than required. The fifth building block strategy details the process by which you increase wealth by decreasing tax liability with proven and legal methods.

**Solution 28: Donate to Churches and Charities**

It is both a wise financial decision and a good moral and social act to donate to churches and charities that provide services to those in need. Since there are tax deductions for contributions to churches or charities, your donations reduce your tax liability.

Donations Qualified for Tax Deduction:

- Cash or check (keep receipts or other reliable written records showing the name of the charity and the date and amount of your donation)
- Property (keep records of the gift's description and value, the name of the charity, and the date of donation)
- Out-of-pocket expenses resulting from volunteer work (keep itemized written records)
- Costs incurred by use of vehicle for volunteer work (keep written records of exact mileage and expenses)

• Trusts in the name of charities (to be discussed in Solution 44 on page 89)

The total of all the above contributions cannot exceed half of your Adjusted Gross Income (AGI) in any one year. Also, do not deduct any expenses for which you were reimbursed.

**Solution 29: Use Timing to Your Advantage**

Effective tax planning involves timing income and deductions so as to reduce or postpone tax liabilities over a period of several years. Most tax planners generally advise postponing income until the next year and accelerating deductions in the current year. However, due to the complexity of the current tax code and changing administrations, this general rule may not always apply.

It is important to consider these five factors:

1. Good tax planning requires accurate estimates of taxable income for the current and coming years.
2. Future tax rates may increase drastically for certain tax brackets.
3. Since 1993, personal exemptions are gradually eliminated over a range of adjusted gross income.
4. Take into consideration the depreciation of money based on inflation in relation to anticipated tax increases.
5. The Alternative Minimum Tax (AMT) must be accounted for in your tax planning. The AMT establishes a minimum amount of taxes to be paid by disallowing certain deductions and exemptions.

If you need to defer income until next year or increase deductions in the current year, you should consider the following actions:

• Your winter bonus check should be dated after January 1 of the New Year.
• Your January mortgage payment should be paid and applied before December 31 of the current year.
• Prepay any additional state and local taxes that may be due for the current year.

- Set up a KEOGH plan before December 31 and an IRA before April 15 of the following year. KEOGH plans are full-fledged pension plans for self-employed people in the United States.

Remember to meet with your tax planner as soon as possible to allow time to actually implement the necessary tactics.

**Solution 30: Stop Giving Uncle Sam 0 Percent Interest Loans**

Many Americans are unwittingly loaning part of their salary to Uncle Sam interest free. If you are one of the many tax payers who receive an annual tax refund check from the U.S. Treasury, you are one of these people.

Often the government appropriates more of your income than necessary out of your paycheck. This is a result of having selected the wrong number of deductions on your Employee's Withholding Allowance Certificate, better known as your W-4 form. Even though you eventually get your money back in the form of a refund, the government uses that money for its own purposes in the interim without paying you a penny of interest.

The solution is simple. Increase the number of allowances by completing a new W-4 form. Remember that the number of allowances do not represent how many dependents you have but how many deductions are taken from your paycheck. One word of caution, if you claim more than nine allowances, the IRS requires your employer send them a copy of your revised form. Since you may have to justify why you have more than nine allowances, be prepared to explain your calculations to the IRS.

**Solution 31: Use a Cafeteria Plan**

The capability to pay for benefits with pre-tax dollars is the fundamental purpose of a Cafeteria or Section 125 plan. Basically, it enables an employer to establish a written plan, which allows an employee a selection of benefits that include group term life, disability income insurance, dependent care, dental insurance, health insurance, and legal services. The employee selects the desired benefits from the menu and determines the current monthly or an anticipated annual cost. If annual, this estimated amount is calculated as a monthly average. In either situation, the resulting figure is deducted each month from the employee's compensation before taxes. The untaxed money can be contributed by the employer, the employee (in the form of salary reduction), or a combination of both. A Cafeteria Plan allows an employee to pay for these benefits that are not normally tax deductible with untaxed dollars.

The following is an example of how a Cafeteria Plan is advantageous to an employee:

| | No Cafeteria Plan | Cafeteria Plan |
|---|---|---|
| Gross Salary | $2,000.00 | $2,000.00 |
| Less Payment of Benefit from Pre-taxed dollars | N/A | $500.00 |
| Taxable Salary | $2,000.00 | $1,500.00 |
| Federal / State Income Tax (15% for illustration) | -$300.00 | -$225.00 |
| Social Security (6.20%) Medicare (1.45%) | -$153.00 | -$114.75 |
| Less Payment of Benefit from Taxed dollars | -$500.00 | N/A |
| Untaxed Salary | N/A | $500.00 |
| Net Salary | $1,047.00 | $1,160.25 |
| Net Tax Savings | N/A | $113.25 |

**Solution 32: Shift Income to Children to Reduce Tax Rate**

The IRS allows parents to shift income to their children in order to take advantage of what may potentially be lower tax rates. Keep in mind that the IRS, under the so-called "Kiddie Tax," requires children under the age of 14 to pay taxes on excessive unearned (check with the IRS for the current amount) income at the rate of their parent's highest tax bracket.

These suggestions offer ways to reduce your tax liability by shifting income to your child:

- *Put Your Child to Work*—If you have an unincorporated family business, it is wise to hire your child for "specified job duties." Employment enables you to deduct the child's salary from company earnings, thereby reducing your tax liability. In addition, if your child is under 18, FICA tax does not apply, although the individual tax rate does.

- *Take Advantage of Gift Tax Exclusions*—You and your spouse can each give up to $12,000 annually to any child or other individual tax-free. Besides money, gifts may include property that is likely to appreciate in value. In this case, both the current value and any future appreciation are removed from your estate.
- *Establish a Gift Trust*—For those parents who prefer not to give the aforementioned gifts to their children, an alternative to direct gift-giving is to set up a qualified minors trust. This plan has the same tax advantages as an outright gift while restricting the child's access to the actual funds.

Additional tactics to reallocate tax dollars
include the following investment tactics discussed
in Building Block Strategy 6 on page 73:

- Solution 35 START A RETIREMENT FUND
- Solution 36 HAVE FUN WITH MUTUAL FUNDS
- Solution 41 BECOME A HOMEOWNER

CHAPTER 6

# Invest in Your Future

The investments you make should ultimately help you work toward your goal of financial freedom for yourself and your family.

The sixth building block strategy focuses on the process by which you get the most return on your investments in proportion to risk. These investments can be as low-risk and practical as buying a home or refinancing your debt, as discussed in Strategy 3. On the other hand, they can involve high-risk, sophisticated investment portfolios. Your advisor will assist you in deciding what programs fit your needs.

When it comes to investing, keep the *FAITH*:

**F**inancial Advisor—Select a proven expert who shares your vision and values. Their job is to work toward your best interest and within your comfort zone.

**A**vailability—Establish the withdrawal conditions, especially the early withdrawal penalty, in case of emergency.

**I**nterest—Find out the guaranteed interest rates. Make sure the proposal is reasonable.

**T**ime—Determine the time period necessary to achieve your goals within a given plan. Be patient, use the power of time to compound your interest.

**H**ow Much—How much can you plan to save or invest? How much risk are you willing to take with your money?

The Power of Compound Interest Over Time:

If Leonardo Da Vinci deposited $1 into a savings account earning 4 percent interest in 1482 (the year of his 30th birthday), his investment would currently be worth more than the Mona Lisa.

The before-tax value of his invested dollar would now be worth over $600 million compared to the $500 million his masterpiece is worth. Furthermore, consider that a penny doubled every day in a month with 31 days would grow to $10,737,417.60.

Even though these examples are extreme, they serve to illustrate the power of compounding interest. As a good money manager with reasonable financial goals, use this power for success.

**Solution 33: Make the Best Investment Decisions**

Considering today's volatile market, your "best" investment is the time you and your advisors (stockbroker, insurance agent, tax attorney, banker, and/or real estate broker) spend developing a well-conceived investment plan focused on achievement of your goals.

This planning is done through a six level decision process:

1. Define Your Current Financial Position.

Begin by having your advisors analyze your income sources and assets in relationship to your expenses, including tax liabilities. They will then make recommendations based on the strengths and weaknesses of your present economic standing. This work is a necessity in order to assure your future income needs are achieved in a tax-efficient manner without significant exposure to principal loss.

2. Identify Goals and Their Timeframe.

One of the most critical aspects of choosing an investment plan is the identification of the timeframe of your goals in relation to your financial position. Once established, you can use the Rule of 72 to help identify the interest rate needed to achieve your investment goal within the specified time period. This rule states that if you divide the number 72 by the rate of return the resulting answer is the number of years needed to double your current investment. For example, if your rate of return is 6 percent, divide 72 by six. This equation equals 12, which means your investment doubles every 12 years.

The Rule of 72 used above illustrates the dependency that exists between achieving your goals in relationship to three variables—time, money, and rate of return. Therefore, less capital and/or a lower interest rate mean that more time will be necessary to achieve a given goal. On the other hand, a greater investment and/or higher interest rate will allow the investor to achieve their goals in a shorter period of time.

3. Determine Portfolio Personality and Risk Tolerance.

The decision level of investment planning is the point at which the "Portfolio Personality," the sum of your investment characteristics (safety of principal, income, growth and risk), is determined. Your risk tolerance in conjunction with the time period needed to achieve specific goals is the key to your Portfolio Personality. Unfortunately, most get-rich-quick schemes and investment plans with high yield potential are also the riskiest. In some cases, the loss could be as drastic as the entire original investment plus all interest. If you are like most hardworking Americans who value their savings, you should consider only safe, tax-deferred investments with little or no risk to your principal and interest.

4. Diversify Your Investments.

The old saying "don't put all your eggs in one basket" applies to your investment portfolio.

5. Find the Best Investment for You.

This decision relies heavily on the investment expertise of your advisors. It is their task to design a program with various investment plans that satisfy all of your goals, personality characteristics, and funding options. However, don't implement any form of investment until you understand the potential risk and have a basic understanding of the proposed venture. Also, learn of any early withdrawal penalties.

6. Establish an Emergency Fund.

Avoid securing all of your funds in long-term projects. It is essential that your overall plan include maintenance of liquid reserves, three to six months' income, in case of emergencies.

**Solution 34: Identify Your Risk Tolerance**

Your risk tolerance is the most important characteristic of your Portfolio Personality, as previously mentioned. This temperament is classified into one of three categories; Low Risk, Medium Risk, or High Risk. The degree to which you can tolerate risk dictates your investment plans.

In order to determine your risk tolerance, decide which of the following statements best describe you:

- *Low Risk*—I don't mind a low rate of return on my investment as long as my principal and earned interest are safe.
- *Medium Risk*—I don't mind risking some of my gain for an above-average return on my investment.
- *High Risk*—I am willing to risk losing everything for the potential of a very large return on my original investment.

Once your degree of risk is established, compare the risk factors of your various investment options with your speculation threshold.

| LOW RISK SAVINGS AND INVESTMENTS | |
|---|---|
| Homeownership | Money Market Funds |
| Savings Accounts | Treasury Bills and Savings Bonds |
| Interest Checking Accounts | Certificates of Deposits |
| Permanent Life Insurance | Fixed-Rate Annuities |

| MODERATE RISK INVESTMENTS | |
|---|---|
| Rental Property | Utility Stocks |
| Long-Term Growth Stocks | Income Stocks |
| Growth and Income Mutual Funds | Variable Rate Annuities |

| HIGH RISK INVESTMENTS | |
|---|---|
| Gold and other precious metals | Collectibles |
| Municipal Bonds | Speculative Stocks |
| Aggressive Growth Stocks and Mutual Funds | Limited Partnerships |
| "Junk" Bonds and Mutual Funds | Commodities |

**Solution 35: Start a Retirement Fund**

*Tactic 35a Contribute to an IRA*

The Individual Retirement Account (IRA) is the tax-deferred personal retirement fund established by Section 408 of the Internal Revenue Code of 1974. Originally, only individuals who were not participants in an employer-sponsored, qualified retirement program were eligible for an IRA, but this was changed in 1986.

Qualified employed individuals can make an annual, tax-deductible contribution to their IRA (except Roth IRA), with some limitations. Employees' ability to deduct their contributions from taxes may be reduced or eliminated if they or their spouse participates in an employer-sponsored retirement plan. Such plans include profit sharing, tax-deferred annuities, pensions, and government employee retirement plans.

There are four basic types of IRA:

1. *Roth IRA*—All contributions are made with after-tax dollars, so your funds and withdrawals are usually tax-free.
2. *Traditional IRA*—Contributions are usually tax-deductible. Earnings growth is not taxed, but withdrawals at the time of retirement are subject to income tax.
3. *SEP IRA*—An employer is allowed to make retirement contributions to a Traditional IRA set up in the name of the employee instead of to a pension plan set up in the name of the employer.
4. *Simple IRA*—This employee pension plan allows both the employer and employee to make contributions.

The way funds are contributed affects their taxation when they are withdrawn. Any benefits resulting from a tax-deductible contribution are subject to income tax later. However, for any contributions made with after-tax dollars the principal remains tax-free while the interest is taxed accordingly.

A 10 percent penalty is applied to the early (before the age of 59½) withdrawal of funds from an IRA, barring withdrawal due to the disability or death of the participant. The penalty is also waived if the funds are withdrawn as periodic income spread over the participant's lifetime.

*Tactic 35b Contribute to a 401(k)*

The 401(k) is the most popular investment vehicle used for profit sharing or distribution of stock bonuses. Under this plan, each employee elects to place a portion of his compensation into this tax-deferred account.

An important feature of the 401(k) plan is the option for the employer to match part or all of an employee's contribution. If the employer decides to match funds the total annual contributions must not exceed certain limitations.

*Tactic 35c Contribute to a 403(b)*

A 403(b) plan, which is similar to a 401(k), is offered to teachers and employees of non-profit organizations.

*Tactic 35d Contribute to an Annuity*

A non-qualified annuity (one which is individual and not employment related) is the best investment to supplement other retirement plans such as a 401(k) or IRA. Basically, this plan is a long-term savings/investment account that provides income at retirement. Even though your contributions to non-qualified annuities are not tax deductible, the interest earned is tax deferred. This means that you pay taxes only on the interest income when you withdraw funds.

This relatively safe investment provides competitive interest rates (either fixed or flexible) for its low-risk status. Fixed rate annuities offer a guaranteed rate of return for the life of the annuity, while variable rate annuities are periodically adjusted to reflect current economic conditions. In addition, part or all of your investment is protected by your state's guarantee fund.

Also, you should be aware that many companies offer artificially high first-year rates that are drastically cut in the following years. However, these accounts are not meant for short-term investment, and early withdrawal is penalized by both the government, in the form of taxes, and your carrier, through penalties.

Early Withdrawal Penalties:

- Early withdrawals are subject to a 10 percent tax penalty, (some exceptions apply) while the portion that resulted as tax deferred interest income is taxed as gross income in the year you receive the funds.

• During the first few years, insurance companies deduct a decreasing scale penalty, as stated in your contract, if you request more than 10 percent of your funds. Most carriers allow you to withdraw 10 percent of your gross accumulated funds annually without penalty. However, tax penalties still apply.

The Fraternal Twin Investments:

Take a look at this example of how time impacts investments. David and Edward are identical twin brothers who do almost everything alike, except when it comes to finances. Consider the following facts:

• *David* begins contributing $100 per month to his annuity at age 27 ½ and stops at age 40 (150 monthly contributions totaling $15,000)

• *Edward* begins contributing $100 per month to his annuity at age 40 and stops at age 65 (300 monthly contributions totaling $30,000)

• The interest rate for the entire investment period for both twins is 3.875 percent

Who has the largest retirement at age 65?

*David's retirement fund at age 65 is $50,824.25*

*Edward's retirement fund at age 65 is $50,657.20*

Even though David only paid on his retirement fund for 12½ years (as opposed to Edward's 25 years), his fund, surpassed Edwards's because it had longer to collect interest. This scenario shows the powerful impact time has on long-term investments.

*Tactic 35e Contribute to a KEOGH*

A KEOGH plan is the retirement plan for the self employed.

**Solution 36: Have Fun with Mutual Funds**

A mutual fund consists of a large pool of investment dollars that are generated from many small investors. Due to these combined assets, the portfolio manager is able to reduce risk while increasing the rate of return through diversification. Mutual funds are, by law, separate investment companies with their own portfolio management and prospectuses. Since this law separates the fund from its parent company, the stability and solvency of each fund is judged on its own merits.

Each plan's unique personality is described in its prospectus, which contains the investment philosophy, guidelines, limitations, and objectives of the portfolio. This direction can only be changed by a majority of the fund's participants via vote. The fund's assets, stability, and past performance records at various intervals are also shown in the prospectus. Never invest in a fund without reading the prospectus.

A wise investor should consider investing in an established, well-managed fund rather than in a new, smaller fund with potential. Overall, most mutual funds are less volatile than individual securities due the diversification of the fund's portfolio. Consequently, fluctuating economic indicators, such as interest rates and stock market swings, have little immediate impact on the assets of the well-managed funds.

Before choosing a specific mutual fund you should consider two measures of performance, the "alpha" and "beta" factors. The alpha factor evaluates specific management risk versus return, while the beta factor assesses the volatility of the fund in relation to the stock market. The higher the alpha number, the greater the management risk. On the other hand, the lower the beta number, the less fluctuation due to market swings.

Mutual Fund Features:

- High return on small investment
- Payroll deduction
- Investment diversification and flexibility
- Ease of redemption and withdrawal of earnings and initial investment
- Inflation hedge
- Instant liquidity through check writing privileges
- Tax-deferred investment potential
- Tax shelter options (IRA, 401(k), SEP, KEOGH)
- Monthly income (automatic withdrawal program)
- Professional money management previously only available to the wealthy
- Volume discounts
- Automatic re-investment of dividends, interest, and capital gains

Mutual Fund Checklist:

- Read and understand the prospectus
- Check the "alpha" and "beta" risk factors
- Examine past performance for one, three, and five year intervals
- Review the diversification of the portfolio
- Determine all fees, charges, and loads (front and backloads)
- Always choose the best managed fund, not the cheapest
- Avoid new, small Mutual Funds

**Solution 37: Reduce Risk through Dollar-Cost Averaging**

A basic technique used by investors to reduce risk caused by fluctuating interest rates and stock price is "Dollar-Cost Averaging." It means a fixed amount of money is invested on a regular basis (usually every month) for an extended period of time (usually several years). The fixed investment buys more shares when the market is down and fewer shares when the market is up. The average cost to purchase shares is often less than the average price per share.

| *Month* | *Regular Investment* | *Price per Share* | *Shares Acquired* |
|---|---|---|---|
| January | $120.00 | $ 8.00 | 15 |
| February | 120.00 | 10.00 | 12 |
| March | 120.00 | 8.00 | 15 |
| April | 120.00 | 6.00 | 20 |
| May | 120.00 | 5.00 | 24 |
| June | 120.00 | 5.00 | 24 |
| July | 120.00 | 6.00 | 20 |
| August | 120.00 | 8.00 | 15 |
| September | 120.00 | 8.00 | 15 |
| October | 120.00 | 6.00 | 20 |
| November | 120.00 | 8.00 | 15 |
| December | 120.00 | 10.00 | 12 |
| ***TOTAL*** | ***$1,440.00*** | ***88.00*** | ***207*** |

Average Cost Per Share $1,440.00 Divided by 207 shares = $6.96

Average Price Per Share $88.00 Divided by 12 Months = $7.33

The difference between the average cost per share and price per share is 37 cents. Therefore Dollar-Cost Averaging enabled this investor to purchase shares at a reduced rate that seems small, but can make a big difference.

**Solution 38: Take More Interest in Your Accounts**

*Tactic 38a Take Advantage of Special Offers*

The interest rates paid by banks and savings and loan facilities continue to be much lower than other investment vehicles, but the risk is also lower, especially when insured by the FDIC (see Tactic 38c, page 83).

The two most popular accounts are regular savings and certificates of deposit (CDs). *Bank savings accounts,* which are insured by the FDIC (Federal Deposit Insurance Corporation), are probably the single safest investment available. Although the interest offered on deposits is very low, your funds are readily available. However, some financial institutions require a minimum balance. *Bank CDs* offer a higher interest rate than a regular savings account, but your funds are committed for a specified period of time. At the maturity date of the CD, the bank pays you the principal along with the stated compounded interest. If you withdraw the funds before the term of the CD ends, a substantial penalty applies.

Although you, as a depositor, cannot control your bank's operations, you can, in most cases, control the overall "effective" return on your deposits by coordinating your many accounts to take advantage of all of the bonuses offered by your bank. These often include: free checking, overdraft protection, credit line with check drafting privileges, low credit card interest, and special senior adult programs. Some banks give rewards when you use your debit card as a credit card.

*Tactic 38b Consider a Credit Union*

In addition to the traditional bank, many large corporations, institutions, and organizations have established credit unions for their employees and members. A credit union is defined as a cooperative group that offers qualified participants saving and loan programs. Usually, these organizations offer attractive interest rates. Therefore, if you qualify to join a credit union, check out both their investment and loan rates before borrowing from an alternative source or setting up a savings plan. In most cases, as a member of your credit union you will be rewarded through very competitive rates.

*Tactic 38c Maximize Your FDIC Protection*

The FDIC guarantees the safety of your checking and savings deposits made in member banks. The 2008 bailout bill raised the amount of FDIC insurance to $250,000 per qualifying account, but this guarantee only lasts until the end of 2009.

In order to maximize your protection for deposits above the threshold, establish accounts at different banks. For example, a person with accounts at two or more banks (not branches of the same bank) can keep $250,000 in each account and be insured for the total. In addition, if a person has more than one account at the same bank with different ownership types (such as individual, trust, and joint accounts), the accounts are considered separately for the $250,000 limit. IRAs are individually insured up to $250,000.

**Solution 39: Buy U.S. Treasury Securities**

U.S. Treasury securities are issued by the government and backed by the full faith and credit of the United States. Interest is exempt from state and local taxes, but not from federal. Because of their safety, demand is high and interest rates are low.

There are four major types of options:

- *Treasury notes,* or T-Notes, which mature in two to 10 years, have a coupon payment every six months. They are commonly issued in denominations from $100 to $1 million with two-, five-, or 10-year maturity dates.
- *Treasury bills,* or T-Bills, which mature in one year or less, do not pay interest prior to maturity. They are sold at a discount to create a positive yield to maturity. T-Bills are considered by many experts as the least risky investment available.
- *Treasury bonds,* also known as T-Bonds or the long bond, which have the longest maturation period, 10 to 30 years, have coupon payments every 6 months like T-Notes.
- *Treasury inflation protected securities,* or TIPS, are inflation-indexed bonds issued by the U.S. Treasury beginning in 1997. The principal is adjusted to the Consumer Price Index. The coupon rate is constant but generates a different amount of interest when multiplied by the inflation-adjusted principal.

**Solution 40: Use the Dollar-a-Day Principal Principle**

The following principle shows homeowners how to turn a $1 investment into thousands of dollars in savings. Start by allocating a dollar a day for investment. At the end of a month take the total and put it toward the principal of your mortgage. If you continue to make this additional payment each month, it will take years off your payment schedule and drastically reduce your interest payment. The example below illustrates the power of just one dollar.

| | |
|---|---|
| CONDITIONS: | AMOUNT FINANCED $75,000 |
| MORTGAGE TERM | 30 years |
| ANNUAL PERCENTAGE RATE | 6.5% |
| MONTH PRINCIPAL & INTEREST | $474.05 |
| ADDITIONAL MONTHLY PAYMENT | $30.41 |

By paying the additional principle, this individual has decreased his mortgage term by 57 months (four years, nine months). This resulted in interest savings of $17,806.62 over the lifetime of the mortgage.

**Solution 41: Become a Homeowner**

The American dream is to own a home. This dream may seem unreachable, but if you set reasonable financial goals and pursue them with focus and determination you can achieve the dream. This is not merely a possibility for your future, it is an admirable goal that would contribute to your financial freedom. Being a homeowner is not merely a point of pride, but a practical and wise financial investment.

Homeownership is a good decision for the following reasons:

1. It is an excellent long-term investment. Even though home values are not appreciating as in the past decades and in too many cases have depreciated, they still function as a good inflation fighter. Rent could fluctuate, but a fixed mortgage payment does not. After all, you have to live somewhere, so why not lock in your payment for shelter for several years. The primary reason

the cost of living increases is inflation. Thus, rents increase with market values. On the other hand, a fixed mortgage remains the same, and homeownership can protect the owner from the impact of inflation. Also, note that as property values increase the homeowner earns equity.

2. The interest paid to your mortgage company is usually tax deductible, which often makes your net monthly mortgage payment less than your old monthly rent.
3. When the house is paid off you'll no longer have a shelter payment as a drain on your income. If you continuously rent a home you never stop making those payments and your total pay out, no matter how low the rent, will be greater than that of a mortgage.

When buying a home or condominium, remember that your decision should not be based solely on aesthetics. This is an important life decision that must be made only after thorough investigation of all the facts.

Here are a few things to watch out for when making this decision:

- Before you purchase your new home or condominium, make sure there are no hidden surprises that could cost you future repair bills. Hire an inspector or contractor to make sure the dwelling is sound prior to submitting a contract.
- Beware of flexible interest mortgage payments. If you must obtain such a loan, make sure it has an affordable interest cap. Understand all the conditions of the loan. Most importantly, this type of loan does not offer one of the major reasons you decided to buy a home—to lock in your monthly housing expense.
- Understand condominium fees. It is important for a condominium owner to understand the condominium charter to determine current and future fee payments. Your mortgage should be a fixed rate, but the fees could one day exceed the mortgage.
- Make sure your new home is covered under an extended home warranty plan. This covers the cost of any repairs or replacement needed for your major appliances and structural damage for a period of up to one year after your purchase.
- In choosing your mortgage company, first determine the

actual (not estimated) total closing cost for your act of sale. The closing cost includes points (prepaid interest), appraisal fees, title search, attorney fees, credit check fees, origination fees (mortgage companies processing fees), and at least one year prepaid homeowners and flood insurance. If you are borrowing more than 80 percent of the value of your home, you will be required to purchase mortgage insurance that protects your mortgage company if you were to default on your loan.

- Shop around to determine if your mortgage company has competitive rates. If the quoted attorney fees seem high, ask to have your personal attorney perform the act of sale.
- Get at least three quotes on your homeowners insurance. (Solution 24 on page 43)
- If you are required to purchase mortgage insurance, any combination of home appreciation or loan principal reduction that causes the total loan balance to fall below 80 percent enables you to cancel this protection, thereby lowering your monthly payment.

CHAPTER 7

# Keep Your Wealth: Estate Conservation

The way we are remembered, our legacy, should be based on more than the wealth we accumulate during our lifetime. It should be based on the love we shared, the gifts we gave, and the unselfish acts of kindness we performed. Regardless, we don't want the fiscal legacy we have worked to create go to waste by a lack of planning. When considering our financial legacy, the way we handle our finances while we are alive will have a direct impact on what happens to our money when we die. Since the preservation of our assets after death can be just as important as their accumulation, the solutions and tactics found in the seventh building block strategy will help us keep our wealth as a gift for future generations.

**Solution 42: Let Your "Will" Be Done!**

In order to ensure that your wishes concerning the distribution of your inheritance are implemented, it is necessary to have a legal document known as a will. By definition, a *will* is testamentary, which means it is a form of covenant. A *will* expresses the intent and guidelines by which to dispose of property and wealth at the death of the testator (male creator of the *will*) or testatrix (female creator of the *will*).

In the absence of a proper *will,* each state has laws that outline a comprehensive plan for the estate's disposal. This plan, known as the *will of intestacy*, has legal provisions for all the possible scenarios in the event of death without a valid *will*.

Congress gave the responsibility of regulating *wills* to each state. Due to the variance of these regulations, it is important that your *will* writer understand your state's laws. Also, since these laws are constantly modified and changed, it is important your *will* be updated to comply with the most current laws. If you fail to do so, your *will* can become outdated very quickly, which may force the *will of intestacy* to apply to all or part of your estate.

**Solution 43: Understand Estate Taxes**

In the past, very few Americans had to be concerned about federal estate taxes, because only large estates were required to file the Federal Estate Tax Return. However, with the baby boomer generation, the most prosperous group in American history, starting to reach middle age, the average estate of middle class Americans will far exceed a million dollars when they reach retirement age. Therefore, the number of estates subject to estate taxes is expected to drastically increase.

Factors for Accelerated Estate Growth:

- Higher compensation and fringe benefits
- Individual Retirement Accounts/Annuities
- Income-tax-deferred savings growth
- Executive bonuses/deferred compensation/profit sharing
- Widespread investment
- Increased awareness of new flexible life insurance products*
- Two-income families
- Impact of inflation
- Emphasis on materialism

**Even though the death benefit of most properly executed life insurance policies is not subject to federal income tax, the benefit amount will be added to the gross assets of the estate if the deceased was the designated owner of the contract. Therefore, the benefit may be subjected to federal and state estate taxes. To avoid this immediate taxation, the beneficiary should own the life insurance policy.*

In 2009, the exclusion amount you can give tax free to your heirs increased to $3.5 million. In 2010, the federal estate tax (but not the gift tax) expires. However, in 2011, the estate tax returns to the 2002 exemption level of $1 million for deaths occurring in 2011 and after.

The allowable deductions used in determining your taxable estate include:

- Funeral expenses paid out of your estate
- Debts owed at the time of death
- Marital deduction (see below)
- Charitable deduction
- State death tax deduction (estate, inheritance, legacy, or succession taxes paid to any state or the District of Columbia as a result of the decedent's death)

*Unified Credit:*

The Unified Credit is the aggregate total of your estate and all lifetime gifts. Any credit used against your gift tax in a year reduces the amount of credit that can be used against your gift tax in a future year. The total of your lifetime gifts reduces the credit that would apply to your estate tax.

*Marital Deduction:*

The Marital Deduction allows assets of an estate to pass from one spouse to another without being subject to federal estate or gift tax. However, these assets will be included in the estate of the surviving spouse, which may push the total assets of their estate at time of death over the current value of the Unified Credit. Proper planning can avoid or reduce taxation. Also, if the surviving spouse should remarry, the situation becomes more complicated.

**Solution 44: Set Up a Trust**

A trust can be described as the personification of a controlling entity that is established by a legal document for the purpose of owning, maintaining, and distributing assets and income. In technical terms, the trust is set up by the "grantor" who provides the assets that are placed in the trust, which is then held and managed by the "trustee" for the welfare of another person who is called the "beneficiary." One of the advantages of properly setting up this entity is to allow the wealth of an estate to be transferred from generation to generation while avoiding the excessive expenses and taxes incurred during the process of probate.

Probate is the legal process in which an estate is administered under the auspices of the court or other designated state entity. This administration of an estate can take several years before all the accounts of the deceased are settled and assets distributed to the named beneficiaries and heirs.

In addition to avoiding the shrinkage caused by probate, trusts are also created to provide lifetime income for children, elderly relatives, and/or anyone who cannot manage their own assets in a reasonable manner. However, the benefactor's inability to control the assets of the trust, which is common to all trusts, is often considered a disadvantage by heirs who are capable of handling their own affairs in a prudent fashion.

Two of the most common forms used to initiate a trust are:

1. *Inter Vivos (Living Trust)* is created and operated by the grantor while they are still living.
2. *Testamentary Trust* is established by the terms of the *will* of the testator or testatrix.

Besides determining when the trust will begin, the grantor must also decide if the trust is to be revocable (the grantor has the power to amend or revoke the trust) or irrevocable (the trust is permanent and final from the day it is created). This important decision may affect how estate and gift taxes are applied.

Under an irrevocable trust, the process of transferring the assets of a grantor to a trustee is considered a completed transaction. Therefore, if the trust is set up for the benefit of anyone other than the grantor, the assets are considered to be a gift to the beneficiary, which are subject to the appropriate gift tax.

In contrast, under a revocable trust, the transfer is subject to change, which means that the transaction has not been completed. Therefore, the gift tax does not apply.

Types of Charitable Trust:

Since only outright charitable contributions are tax deductible, individuals should take advantage of a trust in order to deduct any other gift that is not a direct donation. These gifts include allowing a religious or charity organization to use and/or benefit from income generated by your property. The two most common forms of qualified charitable trusts are the Charitable Lead Trust and the Charitable Remainder Trust.

1. Charitable Lead / Income Trust
   This trust is designed to provide a charity with the income generated from an investment vehicle or a designated property that is assigned to the trust for a specific period of time. The trust will be discontinued at the end of this period, with the ownership of the property, previously held by the trust, reverting to another benefactor such as an heir or heirs. Under this trust, the grantor of the property is allowed to deduct an amount equal to the present value of the future income that will be provided to the charity.
2. Charitable Remainder Trust
   Unlike the Lead Trust, income generated from an investment vehicle or designated property held by the trust is paid to a non-charitable beneficiary. After this period expires, the remaining income is then paid to a qualifying charity. In this case, the grantor is allowed a deduction for a charitable contribution that is equal to the value of the remaining income that will eventually go to the charity.

If creating a charitable trust appears to be a way to increase your giving while reducing your tax burden, consult an experienced attorney who can coordinate your plan.

# Financial Freedom Planner

| Lifestyle | Expense |
|---|---|
| Education | |
| Leisure / Entertain | |
| Grooming | |
| Clubs | |
| Health / Fitness | |
| TOTAL | |

| Savings / Investments | Expense |
|---|---|
| Regular Savings | |
| Emergency Funds | |
| Life, Disability Insurance | |
| Retirement | |
| Investments | |
| TOTAL | |

| Luxuries | |
|---|---|

| Necessities | Expense |
|---|---|
| Food | |
| Clothing | |
| Furnishings | |
| Medical | |
| Staples | |
| TOTAL | |

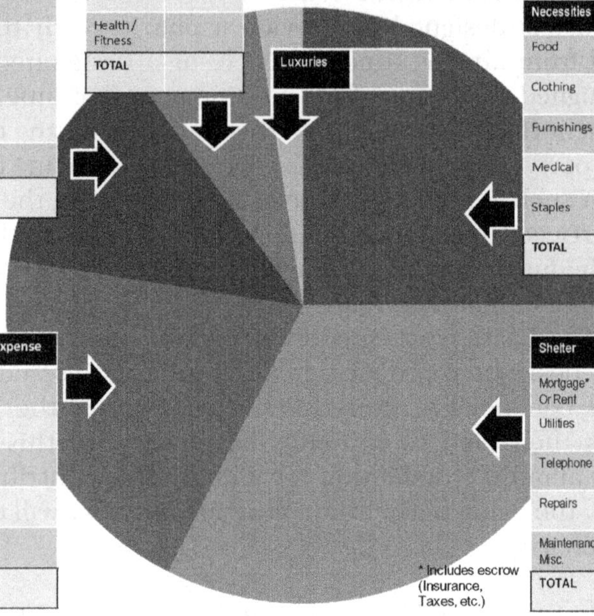

| Transportation | Expense |
|---|---|
| Vehicle(s) Payment | |
| Gasoline | |
| Vehicle Insurance | |
| Repairs | |
| Maintenance / Misc. | |
| TOTAL | |

| Shelter | Expense |
|---|---|
| Mortgage* Or Rent | |
| Utilities | |
| Telephone | |
| Repairs | |
| Maintenance / Misc. | |
| TOTAL | |

* Includes escrow (Insurance, Taxes, etc.)

**Notes**

CONCLUSION

# Discover the Rainbow of Financial Freedom

An old Irish legend tells of the leprechaun's pot of gold waiting at the end of the rainbow. Although this mythical locale has proven elusive to those who seek it, our own pot of gold—financial freedom—is waiting for us.

A rainbow is a meteorological phenomenon that appears as a multicolored arc in the sky; it is an optical illusion. It occurs when the sun shines on droplets of moisture in the atmosphere, usually after rain. The location of the rainbow, with its continuous spectrum of colors, depends on the perspective of the viewer. As the spectator walks toward what appears to be the end of the rainbow, it moves further away.

However, don't be discouraged by this optical illusion. Even though at times our pot of gold, financial freedom, appears to be as elusive as the leprechaun's treasure, we can, through commitment, discipline, guidance, and *44 EZ Solutions,* create a life overflowing with the brilliant spectrum of joyful riches.

The solution to finding the rainbow that leads to financial freedom starts with a decision. It is up to you. Do you decide to keep living a life filled with money woes, or do you elect to discover the peace and joy of being free from financial bondage? If you choose the latter, you can start on the road to financial victory by implementing a few of the tips found in this book.

After all, a solution is defined as an answer to a problem. The *44 EZ Solutions* with its Seven Building Block Strategies and tactics has offered you the answers to many of your financial problems. If you sincerely want to change, you must stop making the same old excuses that keep you trapped by past financial failures. You can't change your past, but you can change the way your past relates to your future.

Do you want to live a life of just getting by?

Do you want to keep living paycheck to paycheck?

Do you want to settle for less than you deserve?

If you want something more for your life, the *44 EZ Solutions* can empower you to overcome the challenges of these tough economic times. These solutions offer much more than information and motivation, they inspire the transformation needed to achieve financial freedom. The rest is up to you.

It is my hope that *44 EZ Solutions to Stretch and Conserve Your Dollar* has stimulated in you a fresh way of thinking regarding your finances. This positive mindset can inspire you to make the right decisions to gain control of your finances.

I wish you confidence, wisdom, and joy on the journey to find your pot of gold. There will be bumps in the road, but despite the setbacks, keep focused on finding your treasure of financial freedom.

# Bibliography


Covey, Stephen R. *The 7 Habits of Highly Effective People*. New York, NY: Simon and Schuster, 1990.

*Electrifying*. LA: Louisiana Power and Light, an Entergy Corporation, 1990.

*Funk and Wagnalls Standard Desk Dictionary*. Harden and Row Publishers, 1984.

*Funk and Wagnalls New Encyclopedia*. Rand McNally & Company, 1986.

Givens, Charles J. *More Wealth Without Risk*. New York, NY: Simon and Shuster, 1991

Gladney, Gerald. *Understanding Insurance*. Stamford, CT: Longmeadow Press, 1991.

Kaufman, Phyllis C. and Stephen H. Green. *Understanding Estate Planning and Wills*. Stamford, CT: Longmeadow Press, 1987.

*Life Underwriter Training Counsel: Business Insurance Course, The*. Vol. 4. Bethesda, MD: 1991.

*Louisiana Update*. Chicago, IL: CNA Insurance Companies, 1992.

Marcus, John. *Tax Bulletin Update*. Metairie, LA: 1992.

Pope, Ethan. *Financial Foundations for Living*. Hattiesburg, MS: 1992.

*Stewardship*. Madison Heights, MI: Parish Publications, Inc., 1992.

Vaughn, Emmett J. *Fundamentals of Risk and Insurance*. New York, NY: John Wiley and Sons, Inc., 1986.

Young, Arthur. *Guide to Personal Finance*. Washington, DC: Conrad and Associates, Inc., 1988.

Made in the USA
Monee, IL
19 October 2026

66036547R00056